MARY ANN UNGER
ACROSS THE BERING STRAIT

April 17 – May 17, 2025

BERRY CAMPBELL

524 West 26th Street
New York, NY 10001
www.berrycampbell.com

CONTENTS

Acknowledgements

5

Pilgrims' Progress: Mary Ann Unger's *Across the Bering Strait*

Glenn Adamson

7

Mary Ann Unger's Microcosmic Monuments to Life

Jess Wilcox

17

Plates

29

Mary Ann Unger, Eve Biddle, and Geoffrey Biddle, Maine, 1989. Photo: Geoffrey Biddle.

ACKNOWLEDGEMENTS

The Mary Ann Unger Estate was founded in 2008 to further the understanding, appreciation, and visibility of Mary Ann Unger's work. Organizing the Estate was originally the vision of Unger's widower, photographer Geoffrey Biddle. The Estate has grown to realize that vision. We have built momentum for Unger's work by leading gallerists, curators, collectors, artists, and art lovers through the Estate, housed at Unger and Biddle's former live/workspace in the East Village. We have placed Mary Ann Unger works into the collections of the Whitney Museum of American Art, the Art Institute of Chicago, and MOCA LA, amongst many other institutions. A major retrospective of Unger's work took place at the Williams College Museum of Art in 2022. This exhibition included work by Eve Biddle alongside her mother's, marking a lifetime of work and family come full circle.

Working as the Unger Estate has given us space and time to have an intergenerational conversation with Unger's work. We both draw inspiration from Unger's dedication to her practice, prolific output, skill with various media, and ability to achieve imposing, yet sensitive, work. The conversations and connections that Unger's artwork has prompted us to have with contemporary artists, curators, and writers have been generative to us both as artists and humans. We are grateful to have Unger's work and practice as a touchstone.

The presentation of Mary Ann Unger's magnum opus, *Across the Bering Strait*, in its entirety for the first time in New York City, along with gallery representation by Berry Campbell, a woman-owned gallery in Chelsea, constitutes a significant milestone—one that eluded the artist during her lifetime.

We began this work by ourselves, figuring it out as we went along, one foot in front of the other, hoping someone would hear us. With this stunning exhibition at Berry Campbell, we are thrilled that Mary Ann's work continues to be part of the contemporary conversation.

We would like to thank the following collaborators who have made this exhibition and catalogue possible: Christine Berry, Martha Campbell, Elisabeth McKee, and the entire Berry Campbell staff, Glenn Adamson, Jason Andrew, Geoffrey Biddle, Adam Eckstrom, Joshua Frankel, Jane Gottesman, Jim Gowans, Brent Foster Jones, Sewon Kang, Seph Rodney, Lauren Smith, Ryan Speth, Jess Wilcox, and Stephanie Sparling Williams.

—*Eve Biddle*
Artist, Co-Founder of the Wassaic Project,
and Mary Ann Unger and Geoffrey Biddle's daughter

—*Allison Kaufman*
Artist and Founding Director, The Mary Ann Unger Estate

Mary Ann Unger, East 3rd Street Loft, New York, 1975. Photo: Geoffrey Biddle.

Pilgrims' Progress: Mary Ann Unger's *Across the Bering Strait*

By Glenn Adamson

At nyght was come into that hostelrye
Wel nyne and twenty in a compaignye
Of sondry folk, by aventure yfalle
In felaweshipe, and pilgrimes were they alle

—Chaucer, *Canterbury Tales*

See her, see her. See her sitting surrounded by the trappings of her artist's life–leather portfolio, cardboard packets bursting at the seams, bits of sculpture lying about, all casual, a gilt frame propped behind her in the window. See her standing in the studio, naked as the day she was born, belly swollen with her own daughter-to-be, Eve. See her, gaze leveled at the camera, a no-nonsense Madonna, bottle-feeding her daughter on the Staten Island Ferry. See her seeming to see you, her piercing eye cocked past the unclad shoulder of her bespectacled husband Geoffrey Biddle, as he takes yet another photo. She is gravely ill, and soon will be gone, aged only 53.

Mary Ann Unger is thrillingly present in these photos, these family snaps which are also works of art, all of which are included in Geoffrey's intimate memoir, *Rock In A Landslide*. They invite us to see her as he did, fondly, desirously, sometimes a little exasperatedly, always filled with admiration for her prodigious energies.[1] The recently renewed interest in Unger's life and career, marked by a milestone exhibition at the Williams College Museum of Art in 2022, no doubt owes something to these portraits. Yet, revealing though Biddle's images may be—vivid, poignant, and true—there is one thing they cannot do. That is to present Unger on her own terms. For that we must turn to her art, which is not still, as photographs are, but imbued with the perpetual motion essential to great sculpture.

Unger's early biography gives ample indication of that impulse. A New Yorker by birth, she had a quick foray in Berkeley in 1967—the year of the "Summer of Love"—then flung herself into travel, taking trips to Mexico, Switzerland, Nepal, Morocco, and the Ivory Coast. When she did settle down together with Geoffrey, it was with some reluctance, and still off the beaten path. They moved into a whole floor

Figure 1. Installation view, Mary Ann Unger, *Across the Bering Strait*, 1992–1994, Hydrocal over steel with cheesecloth and pigment, 72 x 660 x 396 inches (182.9 x 1676.4 x 1005.8 cm), Williams College Museum of Art, Williamstown, Massachusetts, 2022.

of a building on East Third Street, which "smelled of oil, had two stall toilets, walls that were pocked and peeling and a disintegrating floor," as Geoffrey recalls, "more factory than residence."[2] (True enough, the space had previously been used to manufacture metal tea infusers.) Later on, there would be a Hudson Valley farmhouse dating to the nineteenth century, with "a drop ceiling, bumpy stucco walls, and AstroTurf carpeting with linoleum underneath."[3]

Money was always tight, motivating Unger to seek public commissions that she considered somewhat alongside her real art, and develop ingenious, inexpensive material solutions to create an impression of mass and solidity. As Eve Biddle has commented, "I think if Mom could have cast everything in bronze, she would have."[4] She couldn't afford that, so instead she worked in fiberglass, coating it in a resin binder impregnated with iron powder, or welded together armatures of thin steel rods, which she wrapped in cheesecloth and covered with a carapace of Hydrocal plaster and paint. These inventive techniques were doubtless informed by her previous experience with ceramics. While in Berkeley, she had briefly studied with Peter Voulkos and Jim Melchert, two of the great experimenters in that medium. Even in comparison to their wild innovations in fired clay, though, her methods were impromptu; here and there you can peer through the cracks and see the hollow cage of wire within.

Unger's whole career was, in a word, *provisional*, a fact that makes the scale of her achievement all the more impressive. Whether or not the material constraints she faced had any part in it, contingency became then a creative parameter; it was, for her, a whole aesthetic. Most of her sculptures explore the theme of mutual dependency. They huddle together for protection, lean against a wall, prop themselves up. Quite in opposition to her public artworks, they are radically site-unspecific. Wherever they are placed, it is as if they were only resting there, on their way to somewhere else.

Unger's hard-won path eventually led to *Across the Bering Strait* (1992–1994, Figure 1, Plate 11), her most ambitious and important work, and one that remains provocative some thirty years after its creation. She described it as "an abstract sculpture about migration…always on the theme of movement in one direction, always suggesting people walking, carrying, in limbo, but moving towards a goal."[5] It is as much a work of choreography as a piece of installation art. The constituent forms, arranged into clusters, are alternately pliant and cumbrous; some stand staunchly from the ground plane, serving as a crutch on which other elements rest, much as one dancer might lift another. When it was first shown at the Trans Hudson Gallery in 1994, this theatrical implication was enhanced by uplights positioned below the sculptures and an ambient soundtrack of "Tibetan ritual chants, eskimo vocal games, and Inuit Indian chants." As Unger noted, "The sculpture is inherently dramatic, but with the addition of music, the pieces become players in a performance."

The title of the work refers to the fifty miles of clear water that divide the easternmost tip of Russia from Alaska. It is as close as geography comes to the Sistine Ceiling: two fingers of land, almost touching, a gap charged with significance. There is a theory that the Bering Strait (named for the Danish explorer who first mapped it) was once a land bridge, crossed first by animals and then by humans in pursuit, the first influx of ancient peoples from Asia to the Americas. The use of First Nations songs in the work's soundtrack underlines the connection; the Inuit, as well as the Yupik and Chukchi peoples, have long lived on either side.

Yet, as her introduction of chanting from geographically distant Tibet indicates, she always intended to make a far more encompassing statement. It was not so much the specific history of the Bering Strait that interested Unger (as one can tell from her confusing description of the ancient passage as a "Mongol migration," which did

Figure 2. Eva Hesse, *Untitled (Seven Poles)*, 1970, resin, fiber glass, polyethylene, aluminum wires, approximately 107 x 94½ inches (272 x 240 cm). Collection of Musée d'Art Moderne, Centre Pompidou, Paris.

originate in East Asia but went in the other direction, many millennia later, and behind an all-conquering army). Rather, she was thinking of the sights always present in a mass exodus: "migrants carrying their tent poles and their bundles of possessions on their shoulders…mothers holding their children, or men carrying their dead home from war." This emotive imagery is touchingly expressed in the lurching, interdependent sculptural masses, which bespeak the reliance of travelers upon one another. If Geoffrey's photographs dwell in familial intimacy, Unger explores a far vaster, transhistorical terrain, in which, politicized claims to the contrary, migration has been more the rule than the exception.

This subject matter positions *Across the Bering Strait* at an intriguing art historical crossroads. Formally, it is clearly indebted to several generations of sculptors: modernists like Henry Moore and Barbara Hepworth, postwar existentialists like Alberto Giacometti, and the "eccentric abstractionists," as Lucy Lippard called them, who dominated the New York scene when Unger was first starting out: figures like Alice Adams, Eva Hesse, and Bruce Nauman.[6] An especially intriguing precursor is Hesse's untitled sculpture of 1970, often referred to as *Seven Poles* (Figure 2), in which elongated, wrapped metal armatures descend to the floor, where they bend like ballerinas' ankles. It is Hesse's last major work, made when she herself was dying of cancer; yet as Lippard wrote, "the artist's intention held no morbidity…there is a fatalistic calm about them, and a humble look of waiting, without anticipation."[7]

The connections with Unger's own work and life are obvious, but she was also responding to a very different moment. She was making *Across the Bering Strait* when the 1993 Whitney Biennial opened, curated by Elisabeth Sussman with Thelma Golden, John Hanhardt, and Lisa Phillips in a spirit of besieged urgency. There was a culture war on, instigated by conservative assaults on the National Endowment for the Arts (NEA), and they responded with an incandescently angry show, focused especially on the politics of identity. Mainstream critics hated it. *The New York Times'* Michael Kimmelman infamously dismissed the Biennial as "sound, fury, and little else," and even the paper's relatively sympathetic Roberta Smith—who would later write an appreciative obituary of Unger—described it as a "pious, often arid show that frequently substitutes didactic moralizing for genuine visual communication."[8]

In retrospect, the 1993 Biennial has gone down as the defining show of its decade, a crucial turning point toward a more diverse and engaged art world. It is a shame that Unger's works—*Deposition/Nature Mourned* (1991, Figure 3),

Figure 3 (left). Mary Ann Unger, *Deposition/Nature Mourned*, 1991, Hydrocal over steel with cheesecloth and pigment, 36 x 54 x 128 inches (91.4 x 137.2 x 325.1 cm). Figure 4 (right). Mary Ann Unger, *Pieta/Monument to War,* 1990, Hydrocal over steel with cheesecloth and pigment, 85 x 61 x 54 inches (215.9 x 154.9 x 137.2 cm). Collection of Buffalo AKG Art Museum, New York.

perhaps, or *Pieta/Monument to War* (1990, Figure 4)—were not included. They would have fit right in, while demonstrating to critics at the *Times* and everyone else that sculptural intelligence is entirely compatible with social conscience. As it turned out, the Whitney would not display Unger's artwork until 2022, having acquired an early sculpture and several drawings from her estate four years previously. Nonetheless, she should be recognized as a precursor to much that has happened since, including the standout work of the 2019 Whitney Biennial, Nicole Eisenman's *Procession*. While more explicit than *Across the Bering Strait*—both in its figuration and in every other respect—Eisenman's composition has the same sprawling scale, rough-and-ready facture, and demotic interest in the migrant experience. The same is true of *The Procession*, by the Guyanese-British artist Hew Locke, which filled the central enfilade of London's Tate Britain, in 2022, with a cavalcade of figures garbed in "an international ragbag of batik, tartan, sari silk, promissory notes, old embroideries, and modern plastics," as critic Laura Cummings has written, with motifs of enslavement and empire woven throughout.[9]

These projects are, in part, responses to the anti-immigrant propaganda that has brutalized American and British politics in recent years. Xenophobia is nothing new, though, and Unger—the proud descendant of German and Russian Jews on her father's side, and Portuguese and Irish Catholics on her mother's—set out to oppose it. "Populations are shifting all over the world today, refugees from battle or oppression," she wrote. "Migration is arguably the strongest force towards the creation of a global village." Like Eisenman and Locke, she created an allegorical procession that can also be understood as a protest march, with its own participants held aloft as signs.

So far, I have interpreted *Across the Bering Strait* much as Unger herself did: as a work that "evokes memories of our primeval history and suggests a continuity between the journeys of our ancestors and our journeys today."[10] While it is necessary to understand the work in this way, though, it is not quite sufficient. For there is also something weird in it, hard to locate: traits that "exist on the edge of recognition and evade identification," as curator Stephanie Sparling Williams has aptly put it.[11] In its original presentation, the uplighting of the work had an eerie effect, making the undersides of the work look like firelit shelters, and casting strangely distended, overlapping shadows across the gallery walls. Visitors may not have known what they were hearing in the gallery, either; they probably felt they had stumbled into some sort of sacred rite. Above all, the sculptures themselves were and remain, open to multivalent interpretation. Some might have understood them as bony fingers or engorged phalluses. Others—like critic Vivien Raynor, again writing in the *Times*—saw "visions of mutilation, of monstrous fungi proliferating in caves," possessed of "an alarming kind of life."[12]

Figure 5. Auguste Rodin, *The Three Shades*, 1928, bronze, 38¼ x 36 x 54¼ inches (97 x 91.3 x 54.3 cm). Collection of Musée Rodin, Paris, France.

This quality of unruly animacy, together with Unger's central migratory theme, combines to render her work *unmonumental*—yet another art historical dispensation that Unger anticipated. The New Museum's exhibition of that title, which opened its current building in 2007, featured suggestively amorphous sculptures by artists like Rachel Harrison, Shinique Smith, and Rebecca Warren, and was intended to "communicate the unease, displacement, and anger peculiar to our times."[13] Once again, Unger's work would have been a perfect fit in the show, despite having been made fully twenty-five years earlier. For she, more than any other artist of her moment, had deeply considered what an "un-monument" might look like.

To fully grasp this aspect of *Across the Bering Strait*, it is helpful to turn to Rosalind Krauss's *Passages in Modern Sculpture* (1977), a book that Unger presumably knew, given its pervasive influence. In brief, Krauss sought to chart what happened when sculpture transcended its traditional commemorative role. Historically, monuments had done two things: mark a specific place and pay tribute to a particular person or event. Modernist sculptors abandoned this dual function for reasons both extrinsic and intrinsic to art. A pervasive sense of cultural flux–solidity melting into air, and all that–had made gestures of eternal homage seem like retrograde kitsch. Meanwhile, abstraction and surrealism, the primary modes of the early twentieth-century avant garde, broke decisively from conventional representation.

All this was well understood as early as 1938, when Lewis Mumford remarked that "the very notion of a modern monument is a contradiction in terms. If it is a monument, it cannot be modern, and if it is modern, it cannot be a monument."[14] But Krauss built a new critical framework around the rupture. Once sculpture is freed from its commemorative function, she pointed out, it necessarily arrives into the space of the real, and by implication, the temporal flow of the everyday: "meaning does not precede experience but occurs in the process of experience itself."[15] Krauss's close critical ally Yve-Alain Bois usefully glossed this concise formula, writing that she exemplified "a movement from a static conception of criticism fixed on the work to an active theory of the perception and modality of sculpture, not excluding the perceiving subject."[16]

If sculptors had replaced fiction with facticity, the art historian must similarly pivot from iconography to phenomenology. Conventional narrative, as the main focus of potential interpretation, is replaced by sculptural process as it is experienced through time. Thus, for example, Krauss argued that the trio of identical shades atop Auguste Rodin's *Gates of Hell* (Figure 5)—all made from the same mold—are like the generic products of an assembly line, possessed of "an unyielding, mute bluntness." Rodin's surfaces, meanwhile, "express equally the results of internal and external forces," with the musculature of the figure merging with the fissured topology imparted by casting.

Across the Bering Strait is a very Kraussian creation—quite literally a passage of modern sculptures. Taking displacement as its subject, the work eschews narrative, offering instead an abstract and generalized experience. As with Rodin, attention gravitates to the sculptures' handcrafted materiality. This may not be bronze, but the surface is every bit as eloquent (the hunched, trudging forms happen to resemble those of Rodin's *Burghers of Calais*). As viewers explore the sculptures, constantly finding new hollows and protrusions, they are folded into the composition, adding their own movement as if in solidarity.

Toward the end of her book, Krauss arrives at the work of Eva Hesse. Placing her alongside postminimalist peers such as Richard Serra, she writes of how "the properties inherent to a specific material could be used to compose the work, as though what was being tapped was nature as a readymade, instead of some aspect of culture…as though attention to that initial change from raw to processed brought her into a sculptural space that was itself extremely archaic."[17] These words could easily have been written about Unger, and if they had been, would have captured something essential in her art. Yet they would also have missed something important—that generational difference between Hesse and Unger that I alluded to above, which can be neatly encapsulated in the fact that one "did not respond to feminist issues and died before the women's art movement really commenced," as the *Woman's Art Journal* once noted, while the other was an early supporter of the Guerilla Girls.[18]

Here is another way to view Unger's position in art history: even as she extended certain ideas from the late 1960s, she was highly alert to evolving conceptions of art's political purpose. Sculpture, for her, was never an entirely abstract matter. The performance studies scholar Shannon Jackson and art historian Julia Bryan-Wilson, in a jointly authored essay, have noted that in *Passages in Modern Sculpture*, Krauss "proves herself to be acutely attuned to questions of duration," an adept analyst of temporal modes, but "the body moving through these various kinds of time in Krauss was more often than not taken to be relatively undifferentiated, presumed to be a universal subject unmarked by race, gender, class, age, sexuality, or ability."[19] Unger did not have that blind spot. Her sculptures always bear witness to gender, in the sense that theorists like Judith Butler have taught us to understand it, as something that is constantly performed.[20]

This is the kind of theatricality that *Across the Bering Strait* activates. The sculptures are like so many characters playing their various parts, with traits that could be construed as male or female, but not in any stereotypical way—just like any group of people, passing on the road. It is a pilgrimage tale worthy of Chaucer's *Wife of Bath*, another woman with wanderlust, who "koude muchel of wandrynge by the weye" ("knew much of wandering by the way"), and had a capacious understanding of the human condition, sexuality very much included. A similarly irrepressible spirit does shine forth clearly in Biddle's portraits; Unger was a woman who understood, deeply, what it was to be looked at. But in *Across the Bering Strait*, crucially, we see how things looked to her. In this masterwork, she conjures the reality not only of migration, but all of life's rich pageant, with its humor and pathos, its burdens and kindnesses, its worst fears and its highest hopes. Today, at yet another moment of culture war, of unease, displacement, and anger, a time riven by border enforcement and starved of imaginative sympathy, no art could be more essential—or more moving.

---

1. Geoffrey Biddle, *Rock In A Landslide* (Berkeley: Working Assumptions, 2022).
2. Biddle, *Rock In A Landslide*, 15–16.
3. Geoffrey Biddle, *Eve and Me* (Berkeley: Working Assumptions, 2022), 30.
4. Horace D. Ballard, Eve Biddle, and Sarah Montross, "Gathering: A Roundtable Conversation," in *Mary Ann Unger: To Shape A Moon from a Bone* (Williamstown: Williams College Museum of Art, 2022), 52.
5. Quotes from Unger are taken from an artist's statement about *Across the Bering Strait*, c. 1992–1995. Mary Ann Unger Estate. (See pages 12–13 in this book).
6. Lucy Lippard, *Eccentric Abstraction* (New York: Fischbach Gallery, 1966).
7. Lucy Lippard, *Eva Hesse* (New York: New York University Press, 1979), 179.
8. Michael Kimmelman, "At the Whitney, Sound, Fury, and Little Else," *The New York Times* (April 25, 1993); Roberta Smith, "At the Whitney, A Biennial with a Social Conscience," *The New York Times* (March 5, 1993).
9. Laura Cummings, "Human History in all its Variety," *The Guardian* (March 27, 2022).
10. "Across the Bering Strait," artist's statement, c. 1992–1995. (See pages 12–13 in this book).
11. Stephanie Sparling Williams, "Where the Body Ends," *Woman's Art Journal*, 42/2 (Fall/Winter 2021), 3–11: 8.
12. Vivien Raynor, "Sculptural Works That Defy the Limitations of Definition," *The New York Times* (May 29, 1994).
13. Laura Hoptman, et al., *Unmonumental: The Object in the 21st Century* (New York: New Museum, 2007).
14. Lewis Mumford, "Death of the Monument," *Circle* (1938), 264.
15. Rosalind Krauss, *Passages in Modern Sculpture* (Cambridge: MIT Press, 1977), 30.
16. Yve-Alain Bois, "The Sculptural Opaque," *Sub-Stance* 31(1981), 23–48: 24.
17. Krauss, *Passages in Modern Sculpture*, 19–20, 37, 272.
18. Joan Marter and Margaret Barlow, "Parallel Perspectives," *Woman's Art Journal* 31/2 (Fall/Winter 2010), 2.
19. Shannon Jackson and Julia Bryan-Wilson, "Time Zones," *Representations* 136 (Fall 2016), pp. 1–20: 8.
20. Judith Butler, *Gender Trouble: Feminism and the Subversion of Identity* (New York: Routledge, 1990).

MARY ANN UNGER
5 EAST 3RD STREET, NEW YORK, N.Y. 10003   212-505-7713

ACROSS THE BERING STRAIT

"Across the Bering Strait" is an abstract sculpture about migration. It is an installation of variable size and configuration, always on the theme of movement in one direction, always suggesting people walking, carrying, in transit, but always progressing towards a goal.

The title refers to the Mongol migration across the land bridge known as Beringia, between Asia and Alaska. The bridge existed up until the last ten thousand years ago, and it made possible migration into and throughout the American continents* "Across the Bering Strait" evokes memories of our primeval history and suggests a continuity between the journeys of our ancestors and our journeys today. My paternal grandparents were Russian and Hungarian Jews, and for me one specific reference of the title is to the Diaspora.

My father's father was the Hungarian Jew, born on the Lower East Side. The earliest story I know about him is that at twelve, he made burglar alarms for his parents and neighbors by attaching live electricity to the door knobs of their apartments. He went on to be an inventor and businessman with over two hundred patents.

Mother always said that Dad was descended from Atilla the Hun. "You can tell by his heavy eyelids," she would say, and I imagined my ancestors roaring out of Asia across the great Russian steppes with fierce eyes, riding massive steeds. My father had a wonderful ability to do things in the real world: electricity, engineering, plumbing, carpentry, mathematics, gardening. I aspired to be like him.

My father's mother came from Russia as a very young girl. Her picture makes her look sensitive, very sweet, and perhaps too delicate. She longed to return to Russia, and she died young. I have always associated her with a deep melancholy and with a connection to the unconscious, which is manifested in my work.

My forebears' trip to America was yet another journey in the saga of the wandering Jew. I feel great pride in the strength and perseverance of my Jewish ancestors, in their inventiveness and creativity, their respect for learning and education, and their ability to succeed in the face of great difficulties.

My mother's parents were Catholic immigrants who settled in Boston, one Irish and one Portuguese, and I feel that I am a true representative of America's melting pot. "Across the Bering Strait" presents a personal mythology that symbolically unifies the disparate origins of this country.

---

* It takes three years to walk from the western tip of Alaska to the southernmost tip of Chile, walking twelve miles a day.

Mary Ann Unger Artist Statements "Across the Bering Strait," c. 1992–1995.

MARY ANN UNGER
5 EAST 3RD STREET, NEW YORK, N.Y. 10003   212-505-7713

ACROSS THE BERING STRAIT

"Across the Bering Strait" is an abstract sculpture about migration. It is an installation of variable size and configuration, always on the theme of movement in one direction, always suggesting people walking, carrying, in limbo but moving towards a goal.

The title refers to the Mongol migration across the land bridge which existed, by most recent estimates, twenty-nine thousand years ago between Asia and what is now Alaska, a migration which spread throughout the American continents.* It evokes memories of our primeval history and suggests a continuity between the journeys of our ancestors and our personal journey. For Unger, whose grandparents include Russian and Hungarian Jews, one particular reference is to the Diaspora.

The units are posts and lintels - uprights which transform themselves into figures marching across the gallery floor, endowing the work with a narrative content. They suggest migrants carrying their tent poles and their bundles of possessions on their shoulders. Though the forms are abstract, they have a distinctly figurative aspect. The posts are torsolike, whereas the lintels are limblike. "Across the Bering Strait" suggests migrants carrying their tent poles and their bundles of possessions on their shoulders. It also suggests mothers holding their children, or men carrying their dead home from war.

The uprights measure from two to five feet high and the horizontals range in size from ten to fourteen feet long. The forms are made of cement with an acrylic binder pressed into fiberglass cloth, molded over a welded steel armature. Pigment is added to the cement either during the process or after. The basic colors are black or grey with some ochres added as a wash on the surface.

There is music which accompanies the piece based on Tibetan ritual chants, eskimo vocal games, and Inuit Indian chants. The sculpture is inherently dramatic, but with the addition of music, the pieces become players in a performance.

"Across the Bering Strait" is about the past, but it is also about the present. Populations are shifting all over the world today, refugees from battle or oppression, hopeful immigrants and adventurers pursuing dreams. They carry their nationalities and their cultures with them just as they carry their possessions. We may have our hopes for an information superhighway and our dreams of an interconnected world in the technological twenty-first century, yet it still the movements of peoples that makes us aware of each other around the world: migration is arguably the strongest force towards the creation of a global village. Just as it made the world larger thirty thousand years ago, it is still people moving, migrating, and even literally walking, that is making the world smaller today.

---

* It takes three years to walk from the western tip of Alaska to the southernmost tip of Chile, walking 12 miles a day.

Mary Ann Unger, *The Well*, Wards Island, New York, 1979. Photo: Geoffrey Biddle.

Mary Ann Unger's Microcosmic Monuments to Life

By Jess Wilcox

A postcard features Mary Ann Unger's first public artwork, *The Well* (1979), installed in a lush green lawn on Wards Island, New York, east of Manhattan. Bottom-heavy, rust-red ovoids join in a ring comprising the cast fiberglass iron-coated sculpture. It emits what a critic describes as a "dusty radiance of terra cotta," in the most literal sense reminiscent of baked earth.[1] Verdant trees in full summer glory fill the ground, partially obscuring the span of the Triborough Bridge. The sense of scale is indistinct and belies its diameter of nearly fifteen feet. One of over a hundred sculptures presented in an outdoor exhibition organized by the OIA (the Organization of Independent Artists) at the Manhattan Psychiatric Center, located on the island, Unger's sculpture plays with the site's relationship to ideas of health through the double entendre of its title. Wellness is a condition humans are inclined to seek by sustenance of the body and mind. Also central to Unger's practice, *The Well* addresses the concept of "nature" through its radial composition, suggestive of botanical growth patterns of leaves and seeds. Unger's statement on the work speaks to her process and influences:

"I drew it [a flat white squash], and the drawing hung where I saw it for many months. I did a wax model, and by then it had become a sphincter muscle, the guardian of all things that go in and out. On the floor, the model began to look like a miniature scene of animals coming to a drinking hole in the desert. And then it grew, the central space becoming deep and inaccessible, like a well."[2]

Unger describes *The Well* almost as if it was a living, evolving being. In her telling the work shifts among vegetal, animal, human, and architectural realms and various sizes, zooming in, out, and under the skin, undermining taxonomic classifications. The form travels from the public outdoors environment into the intimate live/workspace. *The Well* (1978/2022, Plate 5) is a bronze cast from the described wax model. At around 18 inches in diameter, the bronze is no more sphincter size than *The Well* is water-trough-size but shares a pluri-potent open-endedness. Unger encourages the viewer's mind to shrink or amplify the forms as she does both in her works on paper, writing, and material ranging from fiberglass and bonded iron, Hydrocal, bronze and painted plywood and aluminum.

Mary Ann Unger with *The Well*, Wards Island, New York, 1979. Photo: Geoffrey Biddle.

While unconditionally dedicated to sculptural practice, Unger was clearly influenced by scientific ideas and imagery, namely micro- and telescopic views of the biological or "natural" world. The work has been variously described as primordial, organic, bodily, and environmental. Biomorphic is perhaps the most succinct description. In interviews the artist proposes that her family of engineers and her aborted college study of biochemistry impacted her art. The remnants of these are visible in her uncanny scale shifts; modular, cellular, and radial compositions; and her dual drawing/sculpture practice. These influences are also evident in preparatory sketches, technical drawings, and her journal entries which range from references to DNA and cancer to theories of evolution and universal metaphysical inquiries.

Two umber bonded iron works similar to *The Well*, *Untitled*, 1976, and *Carbon Swell, Kekulé's Dream, Hexagonal Ring* (c. 1978–1980), more directly draw on Unger's biochemical perspective. The latter references August Kekulé, one of the founders of modern-day organic chemistry (a fundamental to biochemistry), who is heralded for his theory of a six-carbon atom ring structure of benzene. Unger's tubular swells resemble Kekulé's "sausage" system for molecular diagramming, in which curved lobes represent valences, its capacity for bonding with other atoms. While the six individual units comprising the work, reconfigurable as either a six jointed circle or a single knobby chain play on carbon's atomic number, Unger's work does not attempt to represent Kekulé's graphic depiction. Rather, the bulbous, repeatable form potentially appealed to Unger for its abstract and elemental character and expansive connotations. Here is a system of "permutations, aleatory inversions and mathematically based algorithms"[3] that she later consciously adopted and articulated via her interaction with the artists affiliated with the pattern-loving Criss Cross Cooperative. Although intended to merge chemistry, physics, and biology into an overarching system, Kekulé's sausage system was widely criticized. The sausage analogy, which stuck, was meant as a derision. These bodily evocations of ground meat and limp phalluses, ridiculed as distractions from the scientific pursuit of truth, may have resonated with Unger's corporeal sensibility.[4] She certainly would have encountered him through her study of biochemistry. Despite the failed diagram, Kekulé still looms large in the history of chemistry, likely due not only to visionary powers and the mythical power of his visions. Kekulé's 1890 attribution of his carbon ring structure to dream of an ouroboros (a serpent devouring its tail) is often cited in discussions of scientific creativity. Such a dazzling description must have struck Unger as generative:

Figure 1. Left: Mary Ann Unger, *The Well*, Wards Island, New York, 1979. Center: Mary Ann Unger, *The Well*, Wards Island, New York, 1980. Right: Imprint of *The Well*, Wards Island, New York, 1980. Photo: Geoffrey Biddle.

"There I sat, writing in my textbook; but it wasn't going right; my mind was on other things. I turned the chair to face the fireplace and slipped into a languorous state. Again, atoms fluttered before my eyes...My mental eye, rendered more acute by repeated visions of the kind, could now distinguish larger figures of manifold shapes: long rows, frequently linked more densely; everything in motion, winding and turning like snakes. And, lo what was that? One of the snakes had grabbed its own tail, and the image whirled mockingly before my eyes."[5]

An avid journaler of her dreams and a follower of mythic archetypes, Unger likely relished Kekulé's story, which may even be apocryphal.[6] Long associated with alchemy, the ouroboros can be traced to ancient Egypt, and symbolizes the union of opposites, the cycle of life and death, and thus an eternal wholeness. The ouroboros of *Untitled (Carbon Swell, Kekulé's Dream, Hexagonal Ring)* exhibits Unger's early inclination for myth, spirit, and ritual–qualities critics typically associated with "private," "personal," and "expressive" studio work of the late '80s and '90s. This provides evidence opposing/undermining the much-repeated narrative of the dual or split nature in her work, which critics frequently mapped onto her public art and "private" or studio practice to differentiate the two. Though an admirer, George Melrod, writing on her public art noted: "Unger's artwork spans such polar extremes that it's sometimes difficult to imagine it all comes from the same creative fount."[7] In a similar vein, the *New York Times* sculpture critic Michael Brenson noted "two sides of her sculpture. The cool and architectural side…" and the expressive.[8] This repeated narrative describes a sculptor who achieved success in systematically playful, architectural public artwork through the 1980s. *Temple*

Figure 2. Two arrangements of Mary Ann Unger, *Carbon Swell, Kekulé's Dream, Hexagonal Ring*, 1978–1980, bonded iron, 6 units (each 32 x 21 x 19 inches) (81.3 x 53.3 x 48.3 cm). Private Collection.

Figure 3. Mary Ann Unger, *Temple*, 1986, painted aluminum, 162 inches diameter (411.5 cm diameter). Collection of the Philip and Muriel Berman Museum of Art, Ursinus College of Pennsylvania. Photo: George Widman.

Eve Biddle and Mary Ann Unger, New York City, 1986. Photo: Geoffrey Biddle.

(1986, Figure 3), a billowing, mushroom-like dome supported by columns constructed in a vermilion planar skeleton, is the iconic work conjured in this telling. In response to her battle with cancer, she created dark, heavy, expressive, and figurative work that developed in the mature and more critically received work of the late '80s and '90s. By then Unger's cancer struggle was well known and ascribed as generative to the emotive, ritualistic, even macabre elements. *Deposition/Nature Mourned* (1991) is emblematic of this so-called latter tendency, consummately described as a "ritual release of innards…that seem dragged from a conventional body to be redesigned in favor of viscera."[9]

The narrative of Unger's dichotomous public and private art practice suggests the deep-seatedness of binary thinking dividing the realms of social (private and public), spatial (inside and outside), consciousness (emotion and reasoning), academia (arts and science), and anthropologic (nature and culture) all overlaid on gendered bodies (man and woman). As noted in Stephanie Sparling Williams' interpretation of *The Well* as an orifice, Unger's interest in mortality and the body's inevitable end preceded her cancer diagnosis (in 1984). *The Well* represents not only a long-standing concern with the existential stakes of sculpture making for Unger, but a nexus of dualistic tensions characteristic of her approach. Indeed, there are remarkable similarities in the public and studio artworks: modular organic forms based on biological knowledge that imply "universal structures of alignment and affinity."[10]

Following *The Well*, Unger's public art trajectory veered indoors with two major projects, both centered on the idea of the garden, occupying buildings with distinct architectural styles and social functions. *Paradise as a Garden* (1981, Figure 4) the site-specific installation at the Graduate Center, City University of New York, was based on the idea of a "formal Baroque garden," intended to be a place for "contemplation, relaxation and refreshment" and an "oasis" in the "spiritual desert" of Midtown Manhattan.[11] Though circular in footprint, Unger organized the installation around a central void, punctuated by five tree-like structures constructed of interlocking plywood ribs and spines. In a vivid spectrum, planes of arches radiated out from the core, conjuring hedge walls and pathways of a garden design. Spanning forty feet in diameter, the installation filled the otherwise dark, drab, lifeless institutional space, called the Mall, which linked the 42nd and 43rd Street building entrances. Unger amplified the threshold aspect of the space by titrating emotional tone through its many modular parts in "a progression of warm and jarring colors on the outside to cooler, more contemplative colors on the inside."[12] Architectural blueprints in plan and elevation (Figure 5) reveal Unger's laborious, blossom-like composition of the hundreds of individual elements—a garden as mandala. The circular efflorescing form is a microcosm of the garden experience.

Tweed Garden (1985, Figure 6) similarly employed a skeletal structure of plywood planes, color gradation to elicit emotion, and abstracted botanical form. The rotunda of the Tweed Courthouse was also a liminal, underutilized space, which Unger likely encountered listed in a City of New York Department of Cultural Affairs guide to exhibition spaces. Declared a New York City Landmark only the previous year, the building is an architectural mash-up. Begun in 1861 under the design of New York architect John Kellum in a neoclassical American Victorian style, it was completed after his death by German architect Leopold Eidlitz, who made significant contributions including many Romanesque elements. A contact sheet (Figure 7) reveals Unger's keen eye for environmental details in the architecture: foliate leaves on column capitals, the bulbous curves of adjacent archways, the octagonal balcony railing, and radial skylight aperture.[13] Like Kekulé's benzene ring and many of Unger's drawings, *Tweed Garden*'s elemental unit was the hexagon. Its root in the biological world was noted: "The columns taper

Figure 4. Mary Ann Unger, *Paradise as a Garden*, 1981, painted wood, 72 x 480 x 480 inches (182.9 x 1219.2 x 1219.2 cm), CUNY Graduate Center Mall, New York.

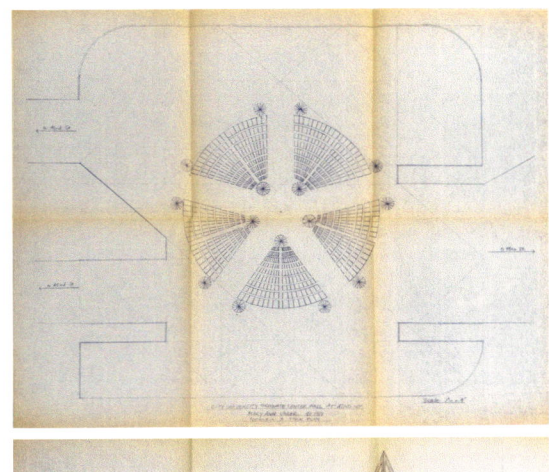

Figure 5. Mary Ann Unger, *Paradise is a Garden,* Floor and Elevation Plans, 1981.

Figure 6. Mary Ann Unger, *Tweed Garden*, 1985, painted wood, 108 x 144 x 180 inches (274.3 x 365.8 x 457.2 cm), Tweed Courthouse, New York.

from bottom to top like flowers or trees—a reminder, perhaps, that columns evolved from trees."[14] The tonal and volumetric shift leads the eye upwards as in Gothic architecture. Likewise, the structure's ample negative space allowed the light through oculus, symbolically uniting the viewers with the heavens, architecturally bridging interior and exterior, and psychically marrying the spiritual and material worlds.

The garden archetype is notable in its inherent boundary-blurring mixing of interior/exterior and nature/culture, brimming with Unger's inclination for "consequential clash." Gardens celebrate the natural botanical world of outdoors, yet connote privacy and interiority. Unger's proposal states the "root of paradise refers to the idea of the garden as separateness—paria (around) and daeza (wall)."[15] Persian garden design in the Zoroastrian tradition conceives of the garden as a microcosm of the universe and a bridge to the spiritual realm. The highly cultivated Baroque gardens of Western Europe exude the impulse to tame wilderness and impose order on chaos. The coexistence of distinct cultural and cosmological perspectives is evident in Unger's journals where a magazine clipping lives beside an astrological chart. Unger's hands-on, embodied experience planning perennial and annual plantings at her rural retreat in Wallkill, New York, complemented these garden designs a metaphysical exercise. Her personal experience of the natural world likely also informed the public artwork both indoors and outside.

If Kekulé's molecular ideas germinated into Unger's earthy ferrous sculptures, and botanical structures informed her garden works, then Watson and Crick's double helix DNA model presented a pragmatic engineered model for the jointed lattice works that became her signature style for public art. A series of related sketches from 1980 on the challenge of designing a monument to Vladimir Tatlin illustrate Unger's biochemical thinking. Tatlin's *Monument to the Third International* (1920) in provisional foreshortened and aerial views are followed by a sketch of the DNA double spiral diagram, which developed into a prototype for public monument-making method (Figures 8, 9). Unger's musings in a typewritten artist statement titled, *Modules*, reinforces the DNA model of the lattice work: "In nature the cell is the basic building block, the Cell is a module and the mold for the cell is DNA. But the mold, in this case, is contained within the form. Matter is not poured into the mold, but the mold, DNA, via RNA, collects its own matter and builds the form around itself."[16] The indoor public works *Paradise is a Garden*, *Tweed Garden*, as well as the outdoor *Temple*, *Beehive Temple* (1987), and later permanent large-scale public artworks *Wave* (1989) in Tampa, Florida, and *Ode to Tatlin* (1991) at the Aaron Copland School of Music in Queens, New York, all employ this method. While similar in their basic methodology, these evolved in materials as her experience and reputation expanded: the gardens were in plywood, *Temple* and *Beehive* in aluminum, and the permanent works in steel.

Unger's movement among materials is ascribable to her lived experience as a woman sculptor, a marginalized position in the art world. Easy to disassemble, pack flat, and produce herself, the planar lattice was a solution to scale up with limited resources. Unger's invention of the bonded iron process was similarly a pragmatic and thrifty solution rooted in the gendered inequality. She cast molds in lightweight fiberglass mixed with iron, which she then soaked in acid to produce the gravitas of weathered steel without the weight. This allowed her to achieve sinuous curves in Corten-steel-color in her studio long before Richard Serra produced his first *Torqued Ellipses* (1998), which he did with the support of computer programming and industrial steel manufacturers. Gender also perhaps explains why Unger pursued public art and university projects. In the '70s and '80s, they afforded women sculptors opportunities that were otherwise limited.[17] Bonded iron's vulnerability to environmental corrosion, exemplified by *The Well*'s decay on Wards Island (Figure 1), suggests another motivation for the shift towards lattice work in the public works.[18]

Unger was aware of the potential illegibility and non-traditional narrative arc of her artistic practice. In journals, she lamented what she perceived as her unfulfilled attempts at triumphal, heroic images. In her struggles, Unger returns to biology to probe the relationship between artistic conceptualization, vision, and creation:

"To Play God! Here I sit in my studio thinking about natural selection—'natural' evolution. [George Gaylord] Simpson says: Nature is an opportunist, if it works then it is good, i.e. it will survive. Sitting in my studio trying one "mutant" after another. Still haven't hit the one that works. Wondering if 'it' has a mind of its own that somehow speeds up the process of creativity like sleeping or divine intuition."[19]

Unger's dual appeal to spiritual metaphor and biological ideas was more readily recognized in some of the studio work of the '90s than in the public artworks. Critics correctly identified whiffs of ancient cultures and traditions, from Stonehenge to Greek myth, that preceded the calcification of binary thinking that emerged from Descartes and has dominated Western European philosophy since the Enlightenment.[20] Regeneration is conveyed not by the round, radial forms of the public works, but through invocations of the biological cycles of motherhood and Earth. In her *Dark Icons*, Robert Taplin noted Unger's parallel "between bearing the dead and bearing a child or seed,"[21] which Arlene Raven also praised as "perpetual compost for the never-ending renewal and residue shaped for the pod of the next flowering."[22] In championing *Black Heart*, one of the ovular convex wall works that Horace D. Ballard has dubbed the *Engagements*

Figure 7. Details from contact sheet of *Tweed Garden*, 1985.

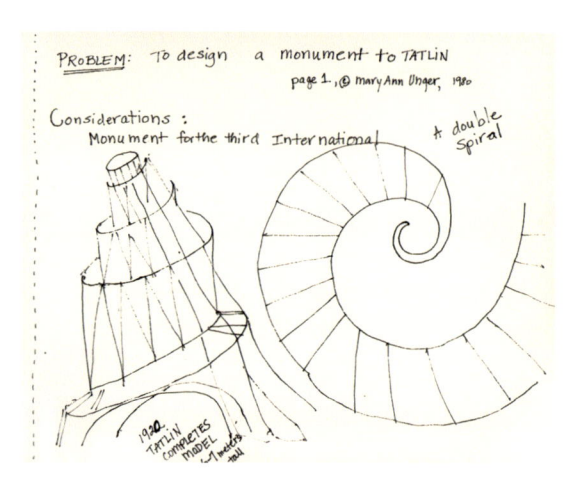

Figure 8. Mary Ann Unger, Tatlin Monument Journal drawings, 1978.

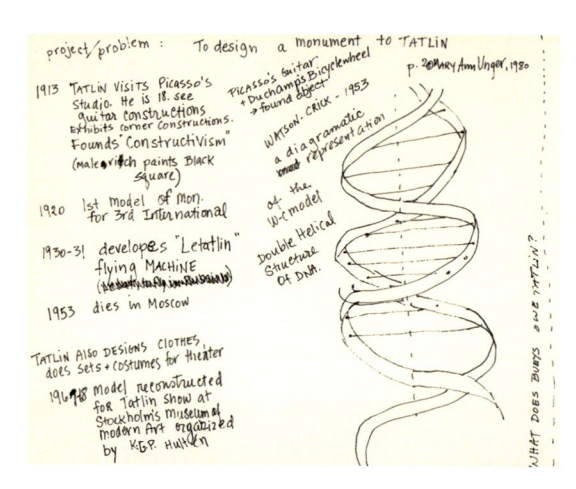

Figure 9. Mary Ann Unger, Tatlin Monument Journal drawings, 1978.

series, Jonathan Goodman contended that while it originates in biology, "its true meaning is rooted in its ability to suggest life processes that are as metaphysical as they are scientific."[23]

The impulse to condense the potency of the universe into fundamental forms is evident in studio work that signals its architectural support. From roughly the same period as *Black Heart*, *Basket Piece* (1997–1998, Plate 22) reprises the radial symmetry and columnar aspect of many of the public projects. Made with Hydrocal over steel with pigment, while the sculpture lacks a uniform surface of the public works, it retains a dynamic play among void and mass. Though suggestive of the capacity to carry, at the magnified height of seven and a half feet, this porous vessel with bulging ribs postures as an abject body. Like much of Unger's work, it leverages a simple elegance in form as a container for multiple open-ended meanings: from ritual totem to chitinozoan microfossils.

Rather than inhabiting the blankness of the gallery, the *Wishing Stones* (1996, Plates 18, 19, 21) protrude outwards from the walls, nonetheless playing with volume and space. According to folklore in Maine, where Unger summered with family, rocks with an unbroken ring around their circumference were good luck. Tumbled smooth by the ocean, the stones encompass the deep time of Earth's lifespan. In deep mineral colors, Unger's lines are reminiscent of quivering horizons: ground meeting ocean, reaching mountain range, kissing cloud shelf. *Maine Wishing Stone No. 3* (1996, Plate 18) could be read as a reflection of the sunset landscape over a dark body of water. Such stones literally compress Earth into a microcosm. They hold the atoms of geological events from the origin of the solar system in the Big Bang through the evolution and extinction of various species, many familiar only through a microscope. Rhyming with an egg, their size echoes a pregnant belly. Seen in this way, the *Wishing Stones* are swollen with potential energy, akin to the *Zygote* (1996) with its titular reference to reproduction.

In the bonded-iron *Misericordia* (1989, Figure 11), originally presented at Socrates Sculpture Park in Queens, New York, Mary Ann Unger's public art development loops around to its beginning. At the monumental size of 8 x 11 x 11 feet, this biomorphic work invites viewers to enter inside and encounter sculpture's full capacity as analogue for the body. Due to its aperture, the architectural scale is more immediate than in *The Well*, as illustrated by photographs of Unger and others inside the work. Like Louise Bourgeois' *Femme Maison* series and Simone Leigh's depictions of black women's bodies in, for example, *Brick House* (2019), Unger mines the trope of women sculptors exploring the female body as architecture:

*This piece is a kind of earth mother gathering her children like the Renaissance image of the Virgin Mary gathering all the orphans under her skirts (*Misericordia*, Figure 10). It creates a protective and sheltering space that is meant to be healing and regenerative. It is like fingers rising out of the ground, or a seed pod unfolding. It is also related to Stonehenge's circle of boulders which makes a ritualistic and ceremonial space. The ceremony is personal and refers to no particular religion or ritual. It is at once ancient and modern. The interior is dark and mute, encompassing some mysterious process of transformation.*

The piece resonated with the site's history: a parcel of land that only a few decades prior was a neglected illegal dumping site, rehabilitated and revitalized by transformation into a public sculpture park.[24] An assembly of eight modules, as if huddled for protection against a harsh environment, *Misericordia* bleeds red from the iron's slow deterioration. Microbiologically, these shapes are most associated with bacteria, which are even classified by the rod-shape as bacillus. Here Unger celebrates bacteria's decompositional powers as inevitable and awe inspiring as the patina on memorials that humans have made since ancient times, to say nothing of Christianity's associations with resurrection. A vital life force is acknowledged equally in the human and "natural" (non-human) world via the mythic Mother Earth. While only temporarily installed at Socrates, Unger made *Misericordia* as a monument to endure beyond her lifetime. It's located at Art Omi sculpture park in Ghent,

Figure 10. Piero della Francesca, *Polptych of the Misericordia*, 1445–1462, oil and tempera on panel, 107.5 x 130 inches (273 x 330 cm). Collection of Museo Civico Sansepolcro, Arezzo, Italy.

Figure 11. Mary Ann Unger, *Misericordia/Congregation*, 1989, bonded iron, 96 x 132 x 132 inches (243.8 x 335.3 x 335.3 cm), Socrates Sculpture Park, Astoria, Queens, New York.

New York, nestled among a grove of trees, a natural home for this cosmic sculpture.

This cyclical weaving of Mary Unger's public work, which is deeply intimate, organic, and emotive, with her studio work, which is also architectural, geometric, and environmental, aims to temper accounts of dichotomy and rupture in her oeuvre. An examination of public art output is germane to any artist making large-scale sculpture for its long entanglement with the idea of the monument, but all the more so with Unger because of her long-standing fascination with the natural environment—from tended gardens to inconspicuous beach stones. An emphasis on Unger's journals should not reinforce the primacy of an artist's intentions over the critical and popular reception,[25] which would amount to a rehashing of the personal versus public binary. Instead, the journals and sketches offer focused specimens, prototypes, and case studies in Unger's artistic evolution, from conceptualization, to the working through real world material constraints, to affective responses elicited by completed work. The conflicts and negotiations among political officials, community stakeholders, commercial interests, and legal constraints that are inherent in public art generate project transformations that may obscure and overshadow the subtitles of Unger's biomorphic sensibility and logic. Thus, the public art only fully reveals itself through the interior studio work—as a synthesis of primordial yet post-apocalyptic bioforms. The ouroboros' eternal cycle of self-consumption and recreation broadly pervades Unger's creations, in sculpture and on paper, through spiraling shapes, rhythmic repetition of structures and symbols, and resonance with biological systems. This potent alchemical symbol for the ordering of the chaotic energy of the world's prima materia harmonizes with Unger's all-encompassing sculptural ambition. She created her own microcosms of life, with the matter of life: the planet in the pebble, mother earth in the egg, decay and regeneration in the garden, and the bios (life) in art.

---

1. Lawrence Alloway, "Art," *The Nation*, July 17, 1979, 28.

2. Mary Ann Unger, *The Well: Artist Statement*, Mary Ann Unger Archives, New York.

3. Horace D. Ballard, "Mary Ann Unger: Influences and Arrangements," in *To Shape a Moon From Bone*, ed. Horace D. Ballard (Williamstown, MA: Williams College Museum of Art, 2022), 27.

4. Not unlike Kekulé's detractors, critic Kay Larson likened Unger's sculpture to "flopping sausages" in a review of the "Dark Icons" show Klarfeld Perry Gallery, See Kay Larson, "Small Wonders" *New York Magazine*, March 30, 1992.

5. David Theodore, "Was Kekulé's Mind Brainbound? The Historiography of Chemistry and the Philosophy of Extended Cognition," *Spontaneous Generations: A Journal for the History and Philosophy of Science* 3, no. 1 (2009): 162.

6. Theodore, "Was Kekulé's Mind Brainbound?" 162.

7. George Melrod, "Bridging Extremities" *Public Art Review*, Fall Winter 1993: 24.

8. Michael Brenson, *The New York Times*, May 23, 1986, https://www.nytimes.com/1986/05/23/arts/art-jasper-johns-prints-on-shows-at-the-modern.html

9. Arlene Raven, "Nothing Stays Still," *The Village Voice*, April 7, 1992, 96.

10. Ballard, "Influences and Arrangements," 37.

11. Mary Ann Unger, *Paradise is a Garden: An Installation for CUNY Grad Center at 42nd Street, New York* (Proposal), Mary Ann Unger Archives, New York.

12. Unger, *Paradise is a Garden* Proposal, Mary Ann Unger Archives, unpaginated.

13. While Geoffrey Biddle, Unger's partner took the photographs, Mary Ann directed the process as part of her proposal research.

14. Michael Brenson, "Weekend Arts," *The New York Times*, December 6, 1985.

15. Unger, *Paradise is a Garden* Proposal, Mary Ann Unger Archives, unpaginated.

16. Mary Ann Unger, "Modules," Mary Ann Unger Archives, New York, 2.

17. While Sorkin's traces avenues of support for women working in land art to universities, residencies and sculpture parks in the absence of institutional and gallery support, the argument serves equally for women artists working in public art. While not congruent, the practices share a great deal in common. See Jenni Sorkin, "Structured Power" in *Groundswell Women of Land Art*, Ed. Leigh A. Arnold (Nasher Sculpture Center, 2023), 72.

18. Unger photographed the bonded iron *Unitliled (Carbon Swell, Kekulé's Dream, Hexagonal Ring)* both indoors and outdoors, which again suggests a blurring of the public and studio work designations. See images at the Mary Ann Unger Archives, New York.

19. Mary Ann Unger, Black sketchbook labeled June 21, 1977. Mary Ann Unger Archives, New York, unpaginated.

20. For a reading of Unger's engagement with and appropriation of non-Western culture see Horace D. Ballard "Power Objects: Forms to Rival the Moon" in *To Shape a Moon From Bone*. (Williams College Museum of Art, 2022), 71–85.

21. Robert Taplin, "Mary Ann Unger at Klarfeld-Perry," *Art in America*, June 1992, 106.

22. Arlene Raven, "Nothing Stays Still," *The Village Voice*, April 7, 1992.

23. Jonathan Goodman, "Mary Ann Unger at Trans Hudson," *Art in America*, October 1997.

24. It is worth mentioning that decades later, I served as curator at Socrates Sculpture Park from 2016 to 2021.

25. There is interesting work to be done on the public reception of some of Unger's university projects including *Paradise is a Garden* at CUNY Grad Center, New York, (which was mistaken for Christmas decorations by some); *Temple* at Ursinus College, Collegetown, Pennsylvania, (the location became a subject of debate in the student newspaper) and *Ode to Tatlin* at the Aaron Copland School of Music at Queens College, Queens, New York.

PLATES

PLATE 1. **UNTITLED** 1976   BONDED IRON   32 X 34 X 78 IN   (81.3 X 86.4 X 198.1 CM)

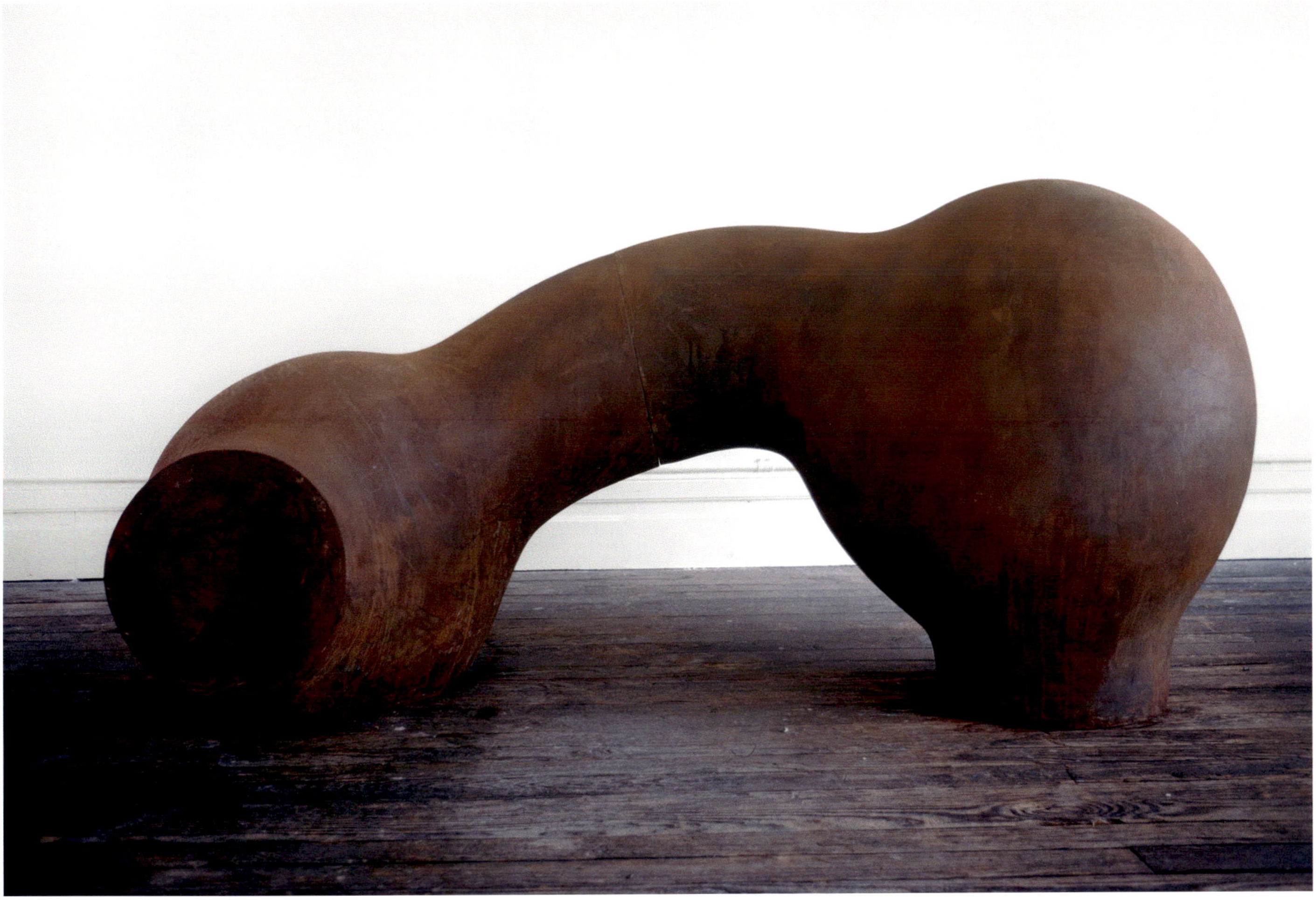

PLATE 2. **PALL BEARERS (STUDY)** C. 1989 CLAY 22½ X 20½ X 12 IN (57.1 X 52.1 X 30.5 CM)

PLATE 3. **JACKS**   1976   STONEWARE   7½ X 14 X 11 IN   (19.1 X 35.6 X 27.9 CM)

PLATE 4. **UNTITLED** 1975 STONEWARE 6½ X 25 X 14 IN (16.5 X 63.5 X 35.6 CM)

PLATE 5.   **THE WELL**   1978/2022   AP 1/1   BRONZE   3¾ X 17¾ X 17¾ IN   (9.5 X 45.1 X 45.1 CM)

PLATE 6.   **UNTITLED (VARIATION OF CARBON SWELL, KEKULÉ'S DREAM, HEXAGONAL QUINTET)**   C. 1978–1980
FIBERGLASS AND COLORANT   6 UNITS (EACH 19 X 34 X 19 IN)   (48.3 X 86.4 X 50.8 CM)

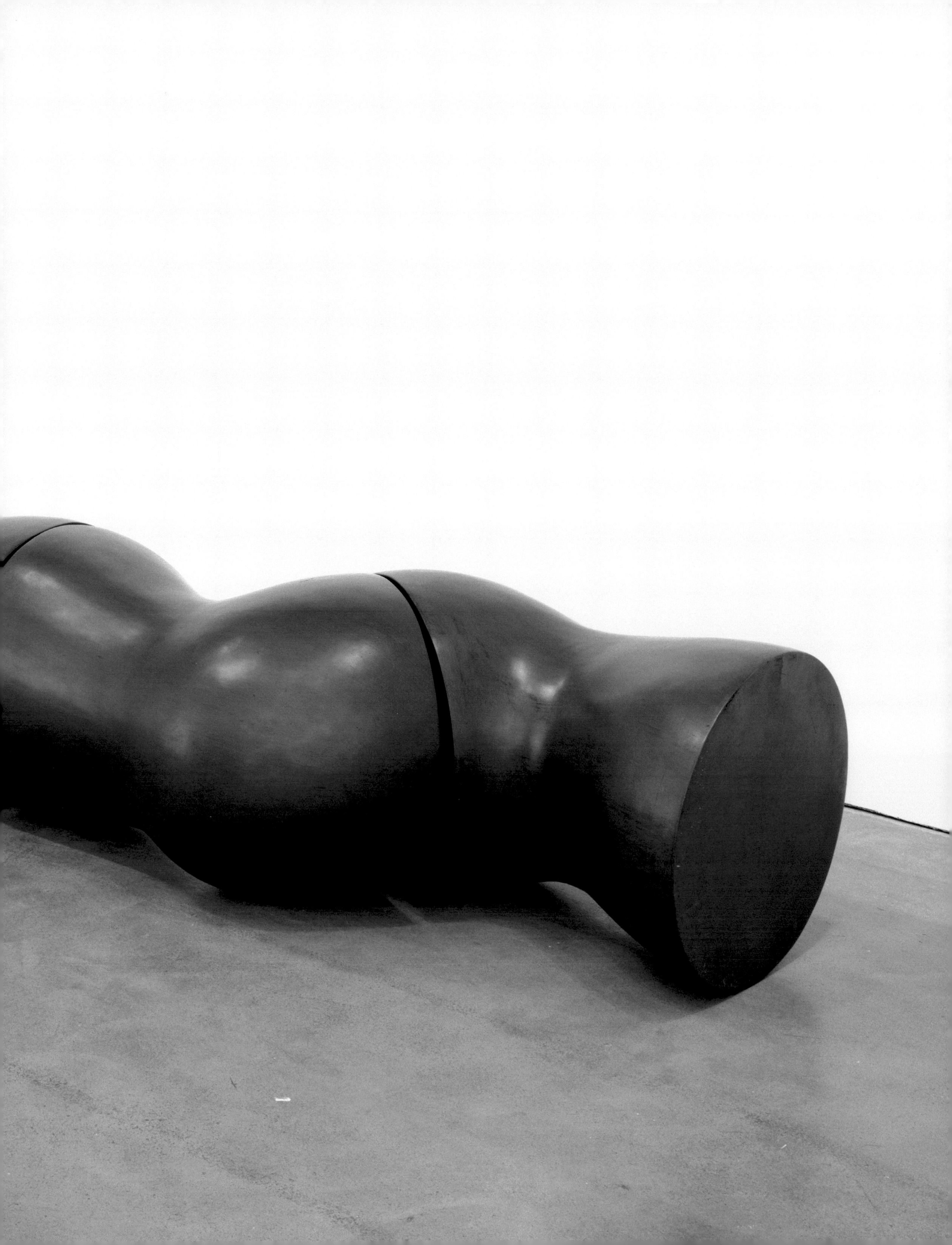

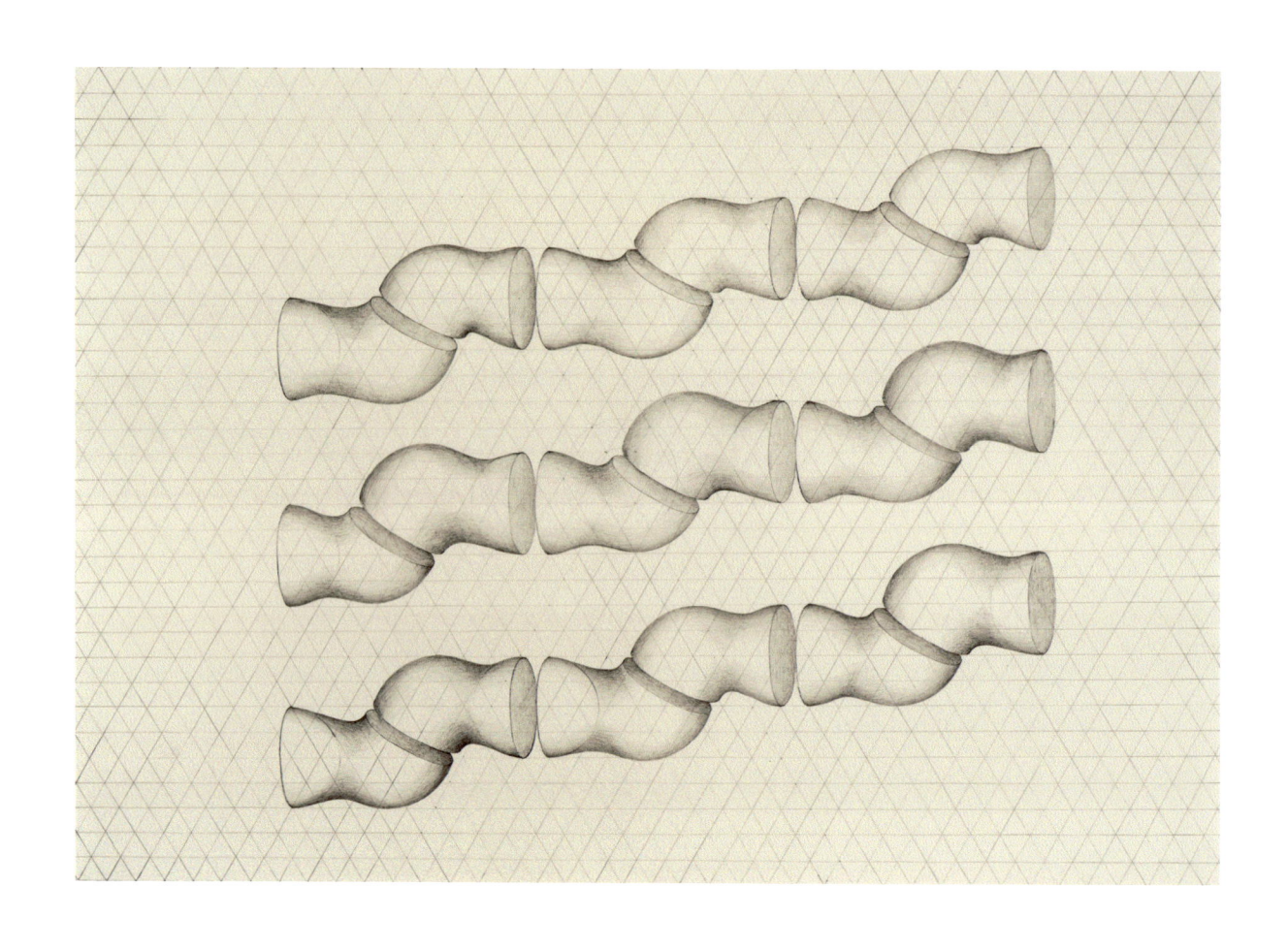

PLATE 7. **UNTITLED (STUDY FOR HEXAGONAL QUINTET)** 1978
GRAPHITE ON PAPER 20¾ X 29⅞ IN (52.7 X 75.9 CM)

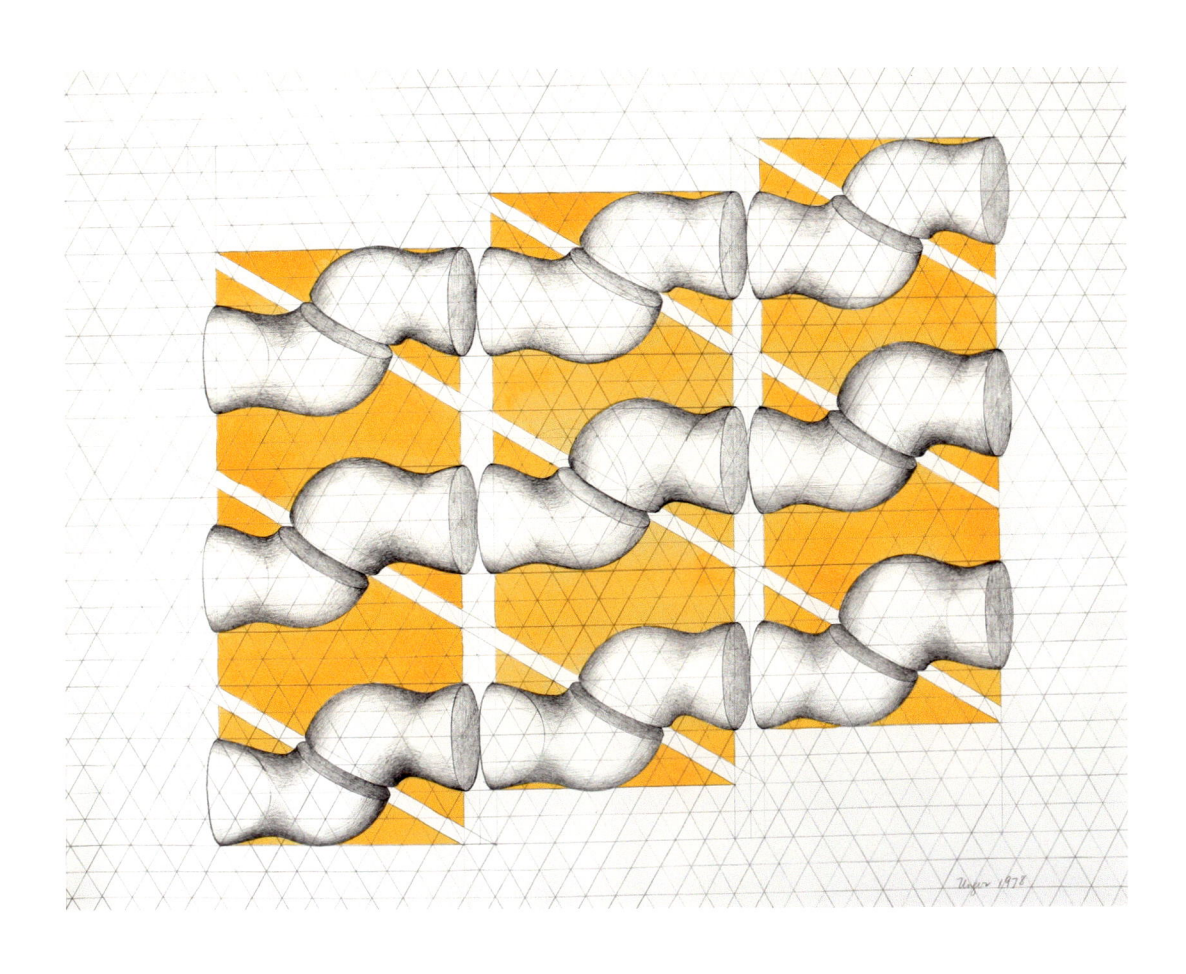

PLATE 8.   **UNTITLED (STUDY FOR HEXAGONAL QUINTET)**   1978
WATERCOLOR AND GRAPHITE ON PAPER   20½ X 26¾ IN   (52.1 X 67.9 CM)

PLATE 9.   **UNTITLED**   C. 1990   CLAY WITH GRAPHITE   7½ X 6½ X 6 IN   (19.1 X 16.5 X 15.2 CM)

PLATE 10. **TORSO** C. 1990 CLAY WITH GRAPHITE 10¾ X 10¼ X 6 IN (27.3 X 26 X 15.2 CM)

PLATE 11. **ACROSS THE BERING STRAIT**   1992–1994
HYDROCAL OVER STEEL WITH CHEESECLOTH AND PIGMENT   72 X 660 X 396 IN   (182.9 X 1676.4 X 1005.8 CM)

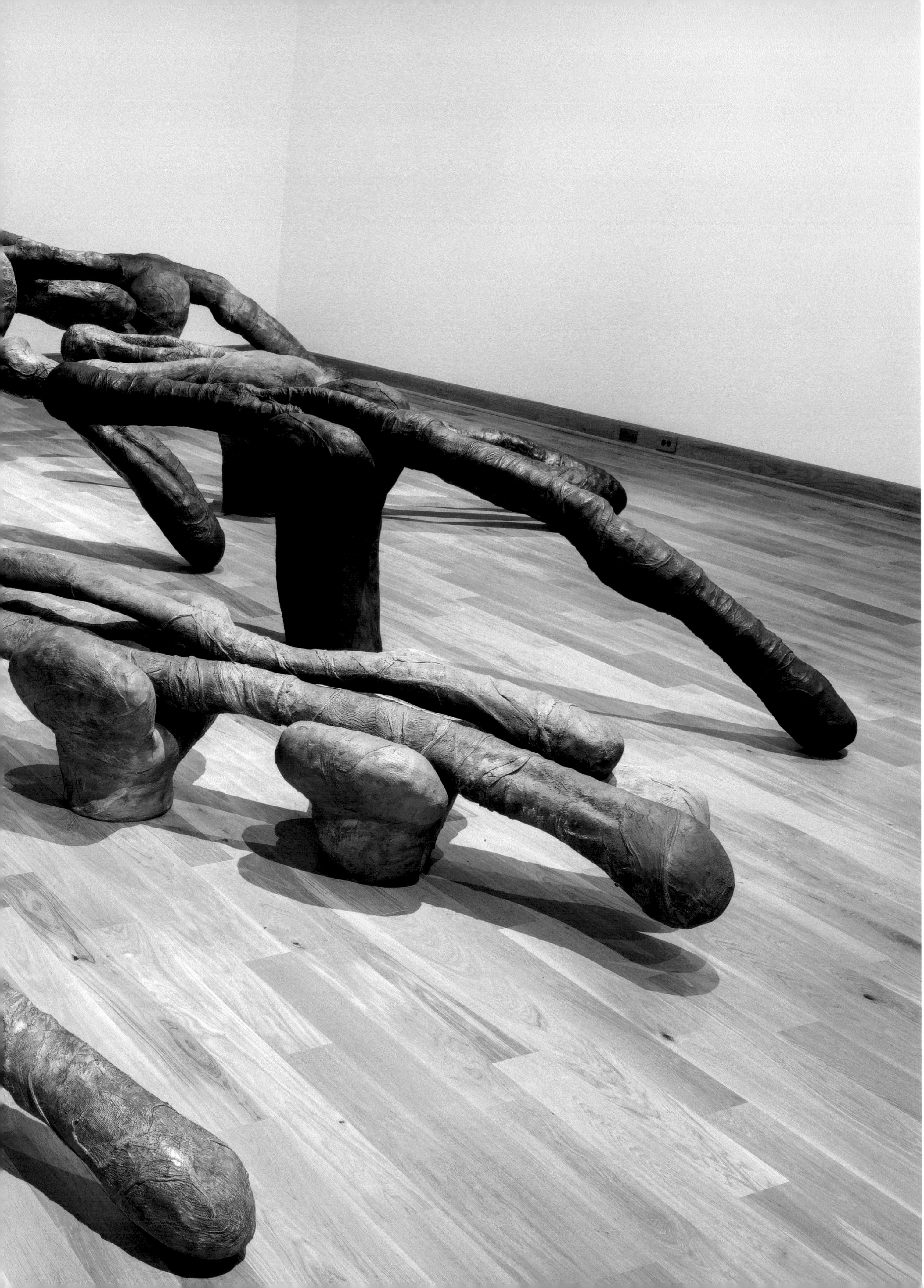

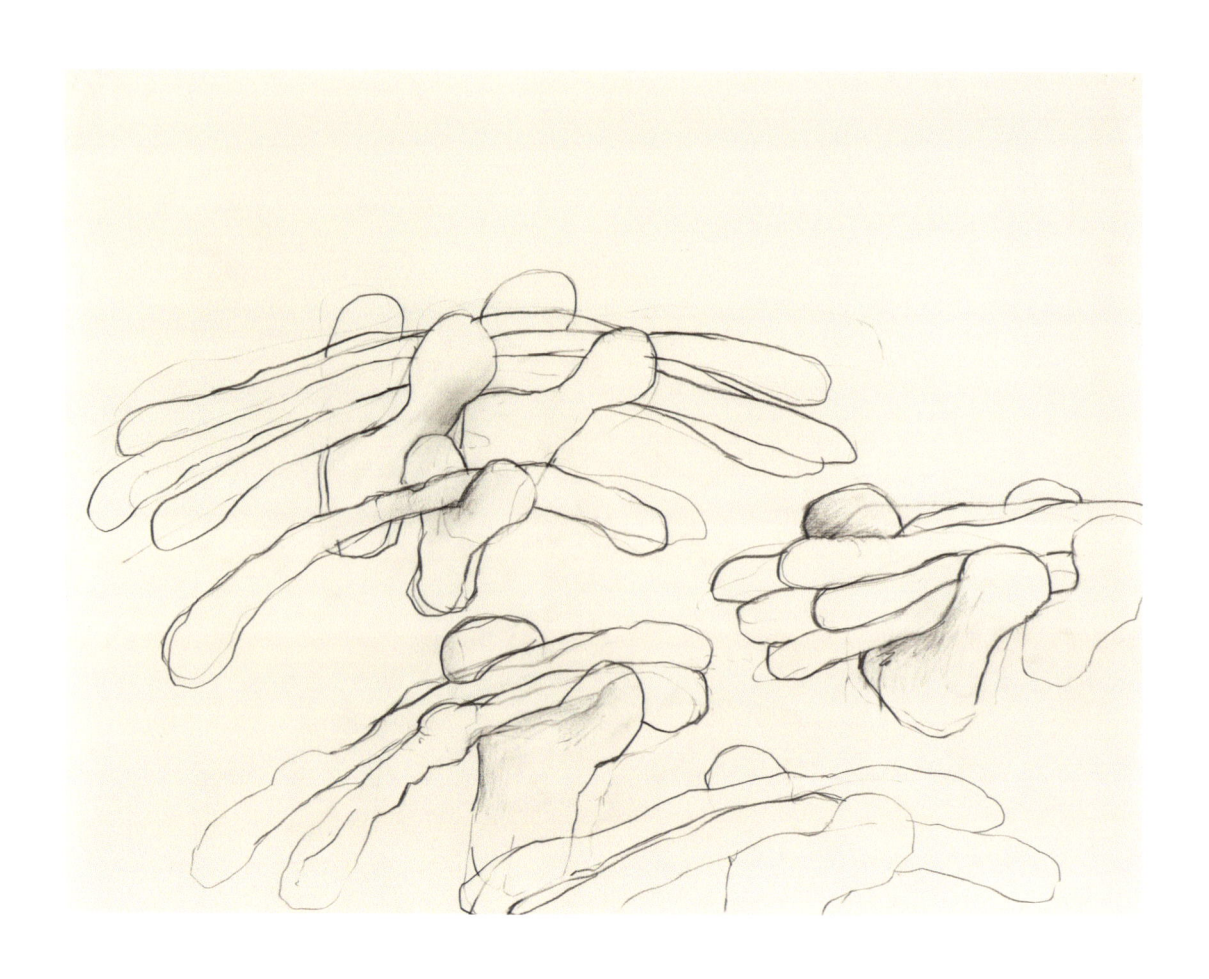

PLATE 12. **AFTER ACROSS THE BERING STRAIT** 1995 GRAPHITE ON PAPER 19 X 25 IN (48.3 X 63.5 CM)

PLATE 13.   **UNTITLED (ACROSS THE BERING STRAIT)**   1996   GRAPHITE ON PAPER   23¾ X 36 IN   (60.3 X 91.4 CM)

PLATE 14. **SEED POD**   1997–1998   HYDROCAL OVER STEEL WITH PIGMENT   66½ X 50 X 6 IN   (168.9 X 127 X 15.2 CM)

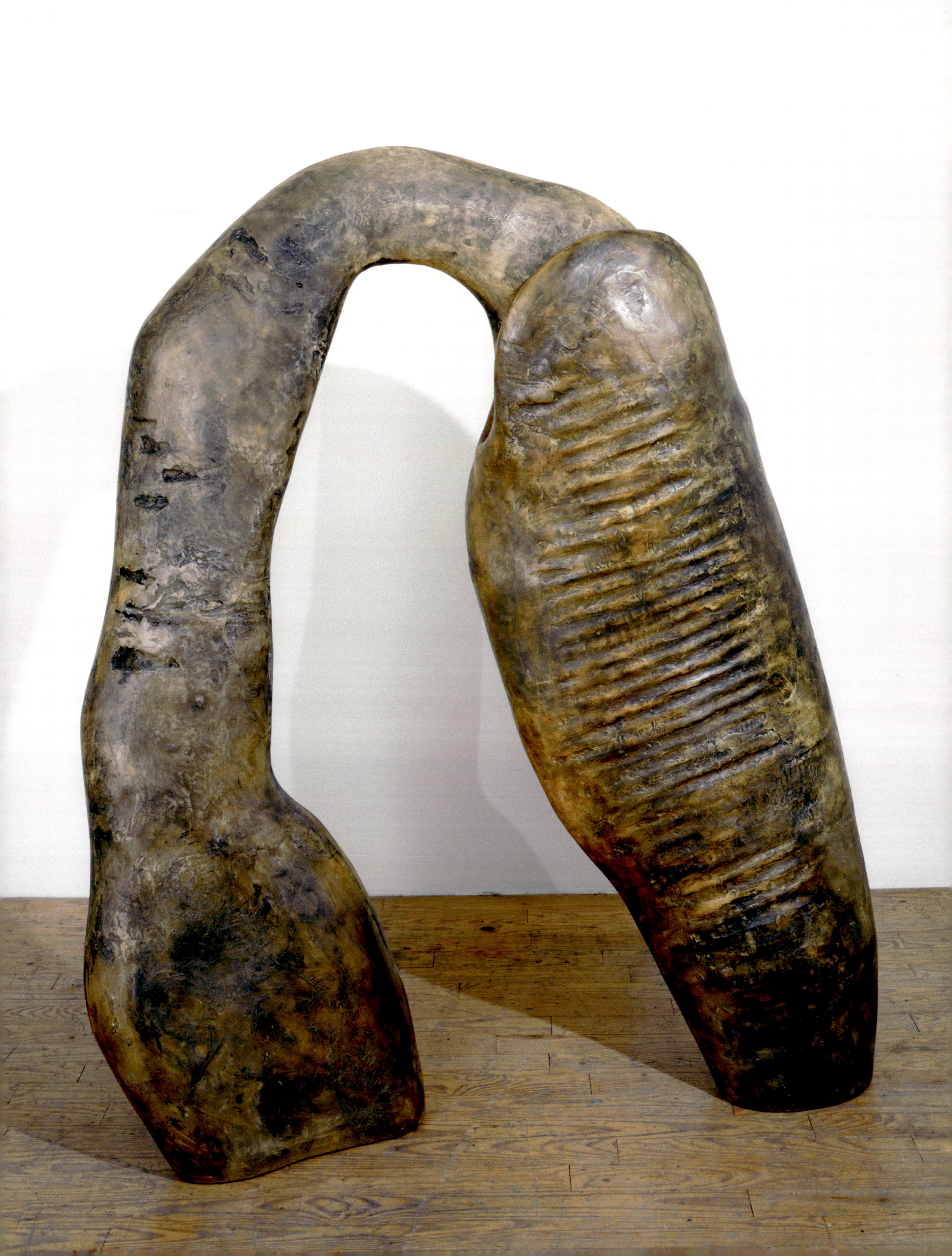

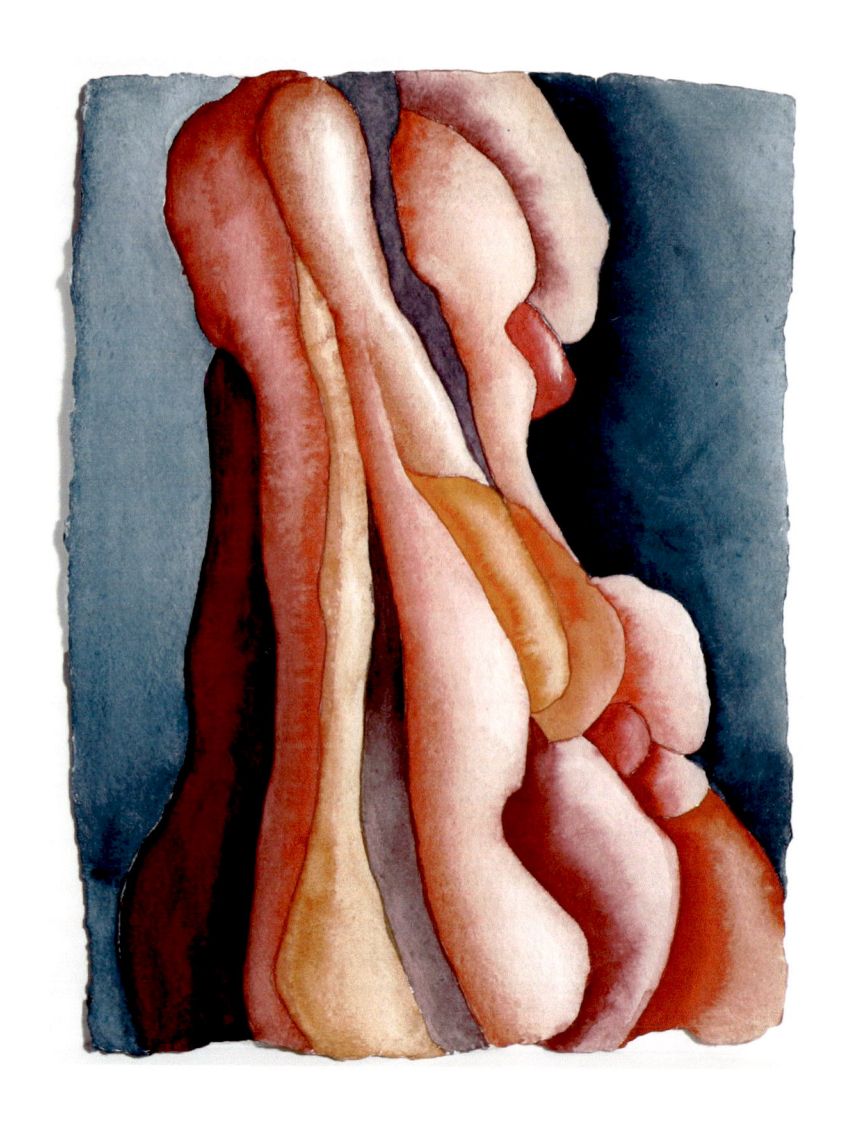

PLATE 15. **UNTITLED (SHADE TREES OF OAXACA)** 1994
WATERCOLOR ON PAPER   12½ X 9½ IN   (31.8 X 24.1 CM)

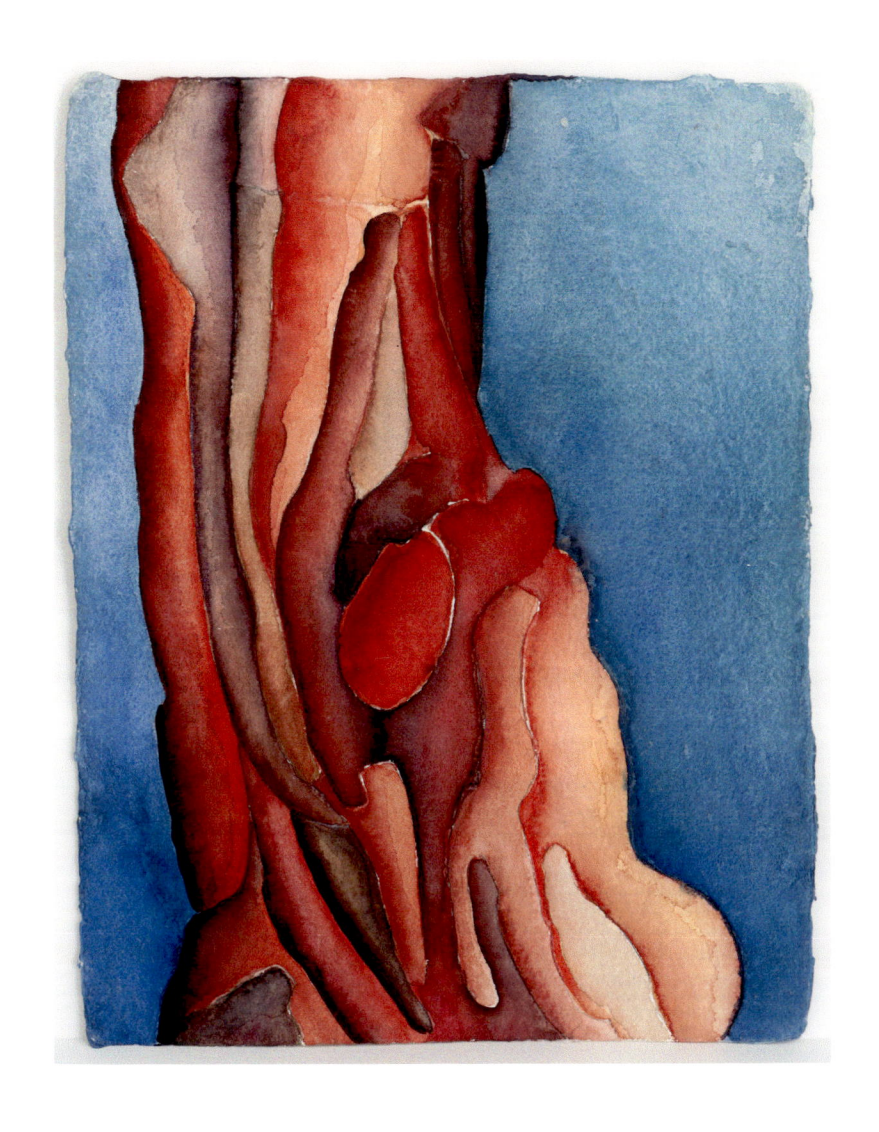

PLATE 16. **SHADE TREES OF OAXACA #6** 1994
WATERCOLOR ON PAPER   12½ X 9¾ IN   (31.8 X 24.8 CM)

PLATE 17. **GANESHA**   1996–1997   HYDROCAL OVER STEEL WITH CHEESECLOTH AND PIGMENT
90 X 32 X 19 IN   (228.6 X 81.3 X 48.3 CM)

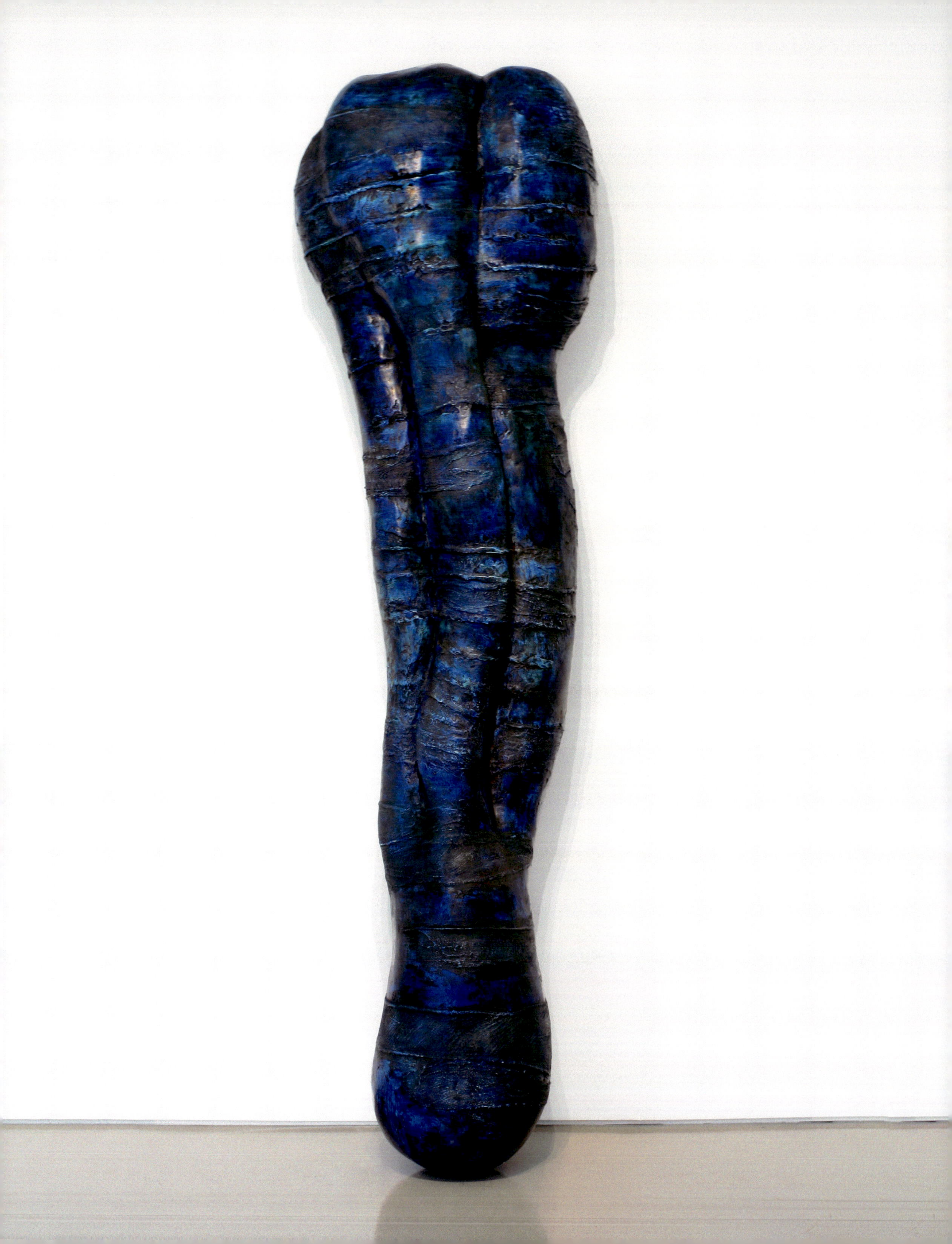

PLATE 18.
MAINE WISHING STONE NO. 3 1996
HYDROCAL OVER STEEL WITH PIGMENT
27 X 18 X 6 IN   (68.6 X 45.7 X 15.2 CM)

PLATE 19.
MAINE WISHING STONE NO. 1 1996
HYDROCAL OVER STEEL WITH PIGMENT
18 X 14 X 6 IN   (45.7 X 35.6 X 15.2 CM)

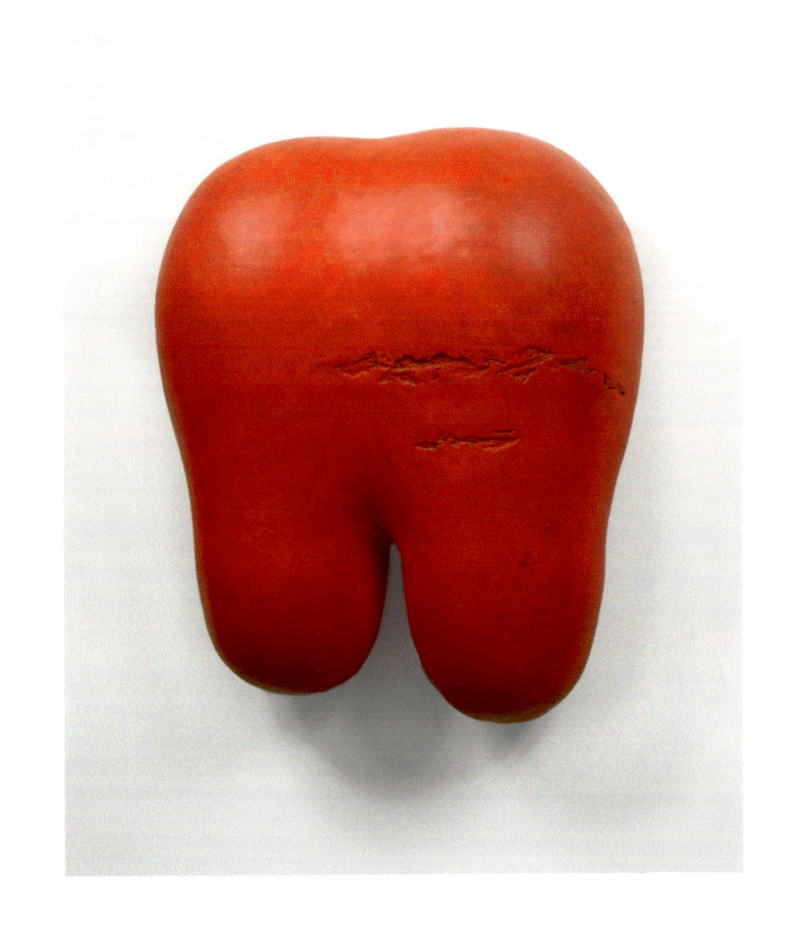

PLATE 20.
RED PALM NUT / RED TOOTH 1996
HYDROCAL OVER STEEL WITH PIGMENT
29 X 26 X 14 IN   (73.7 X 66 X 35.6 CM)

PLATE 21.
MAINE WISHING STONE 1996
HYDROCAL OVER STEEL WITH PIGMENT
24 X 17½ X 4 IN   (61 X 44.5 X 10.2 CM)

PLATE 22. **BASKET PIECE**   1997–1998   HYDROCAL OVER STEEL WITH PIGMENT   89 X 35 X 45 IN   (226.1 X 88.9 X 114.3 CM)

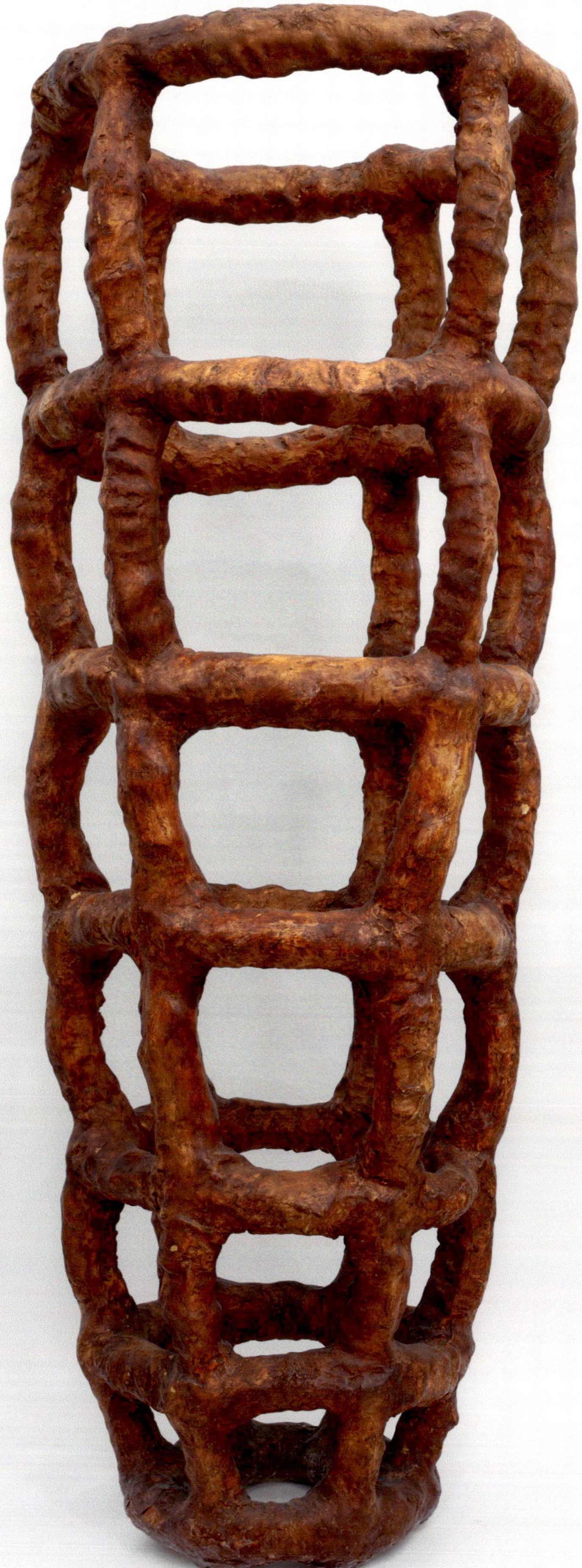

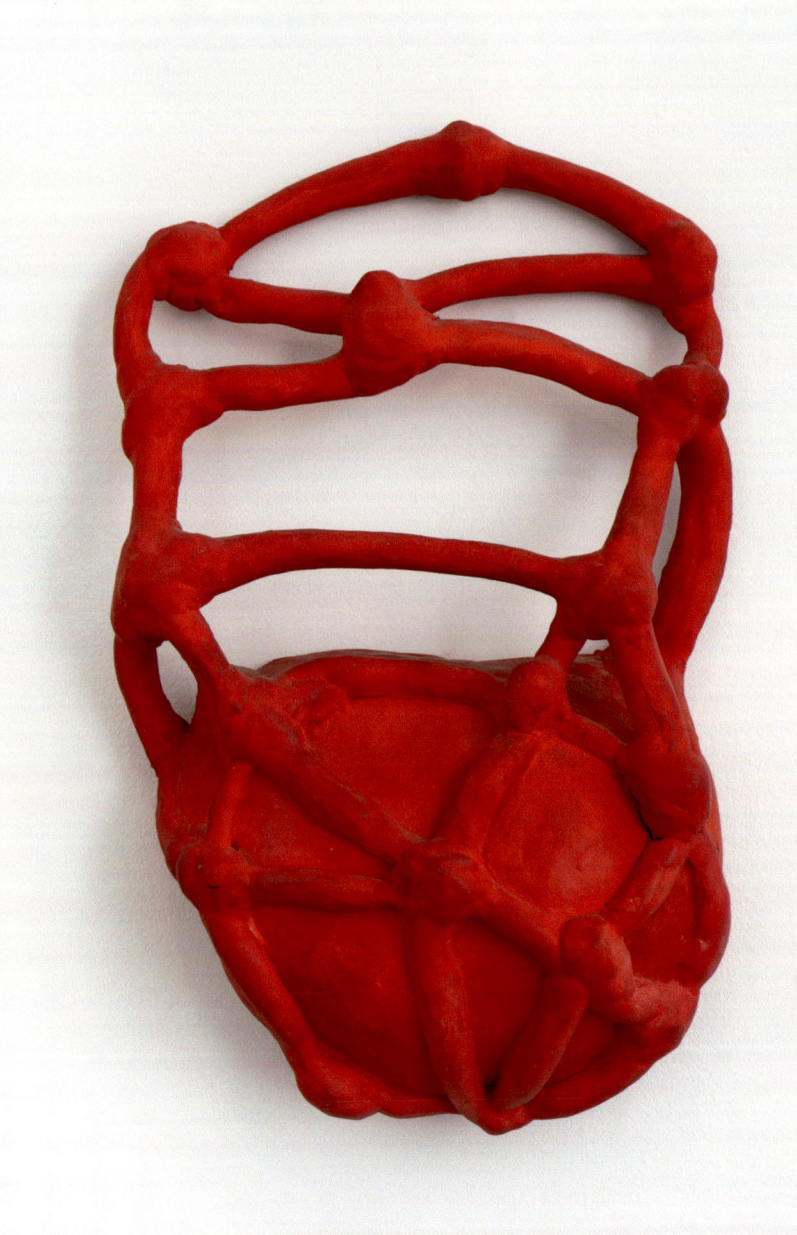

PLATE 23. **UNTITLED**   1997   CLAY WITH PIGMENT   12¼ X 8 X 3 IN   (31.1 X 20.3 X 7.6 CM)

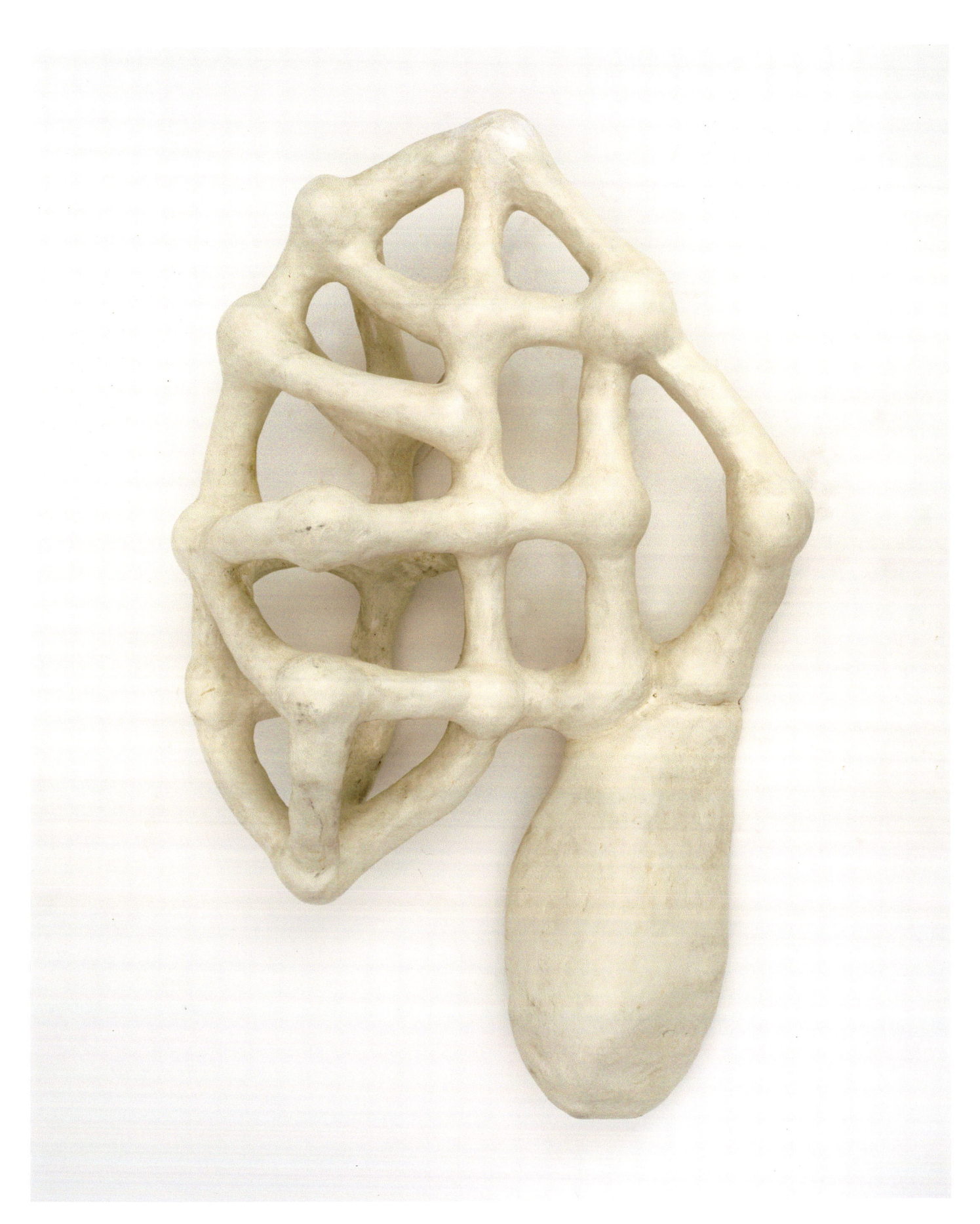

PLATE 24.   **UNTITLED**   C. 1997   HYDROCAL   43 X 29 X 14 IN   (109.2 X 73.7 X 35.6 CM)

PLATE 25. **UNTITLED**   C. 1997   HYDROCAL WITH PIGMENT   48 X 29 X 13 IN   (121.9 X 73.7 X 33 CM)

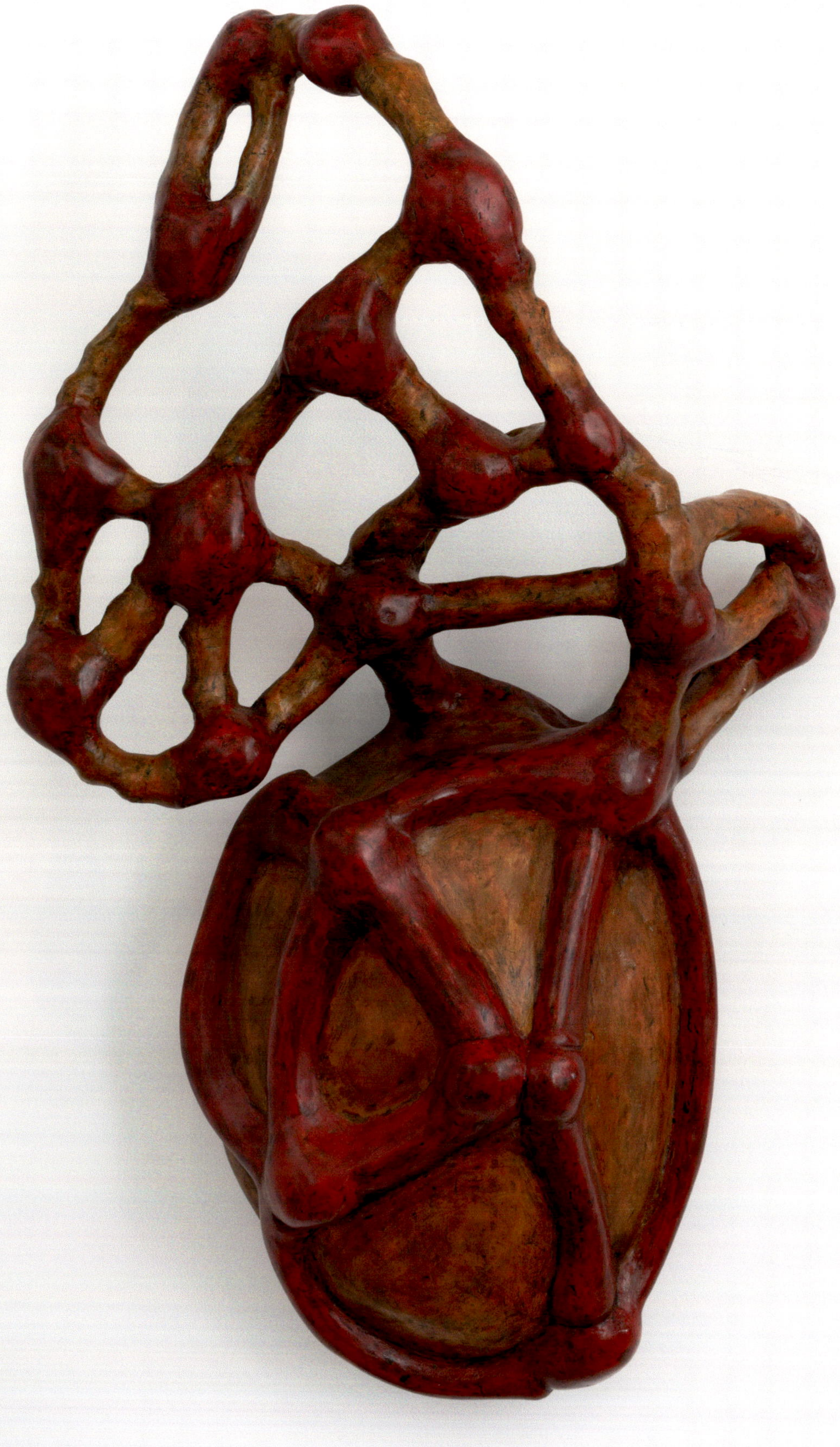

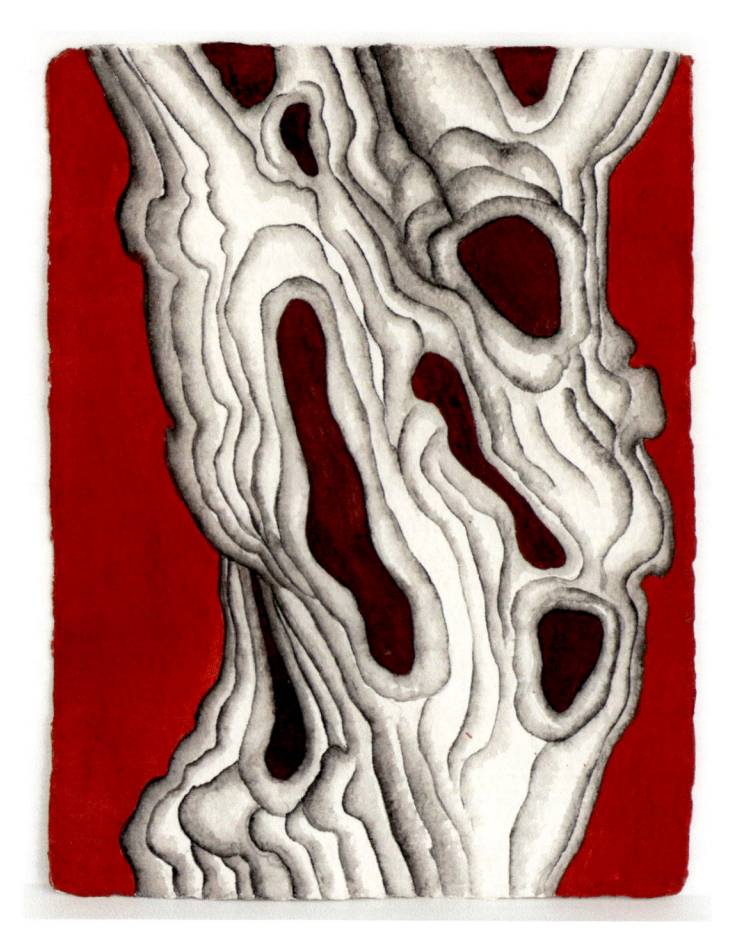

PLATE 26.
OLD APPLE I 1995
WATERCOLOR ON PAPER
12½ X 9½ IN (31.8 X 24.1 CM)

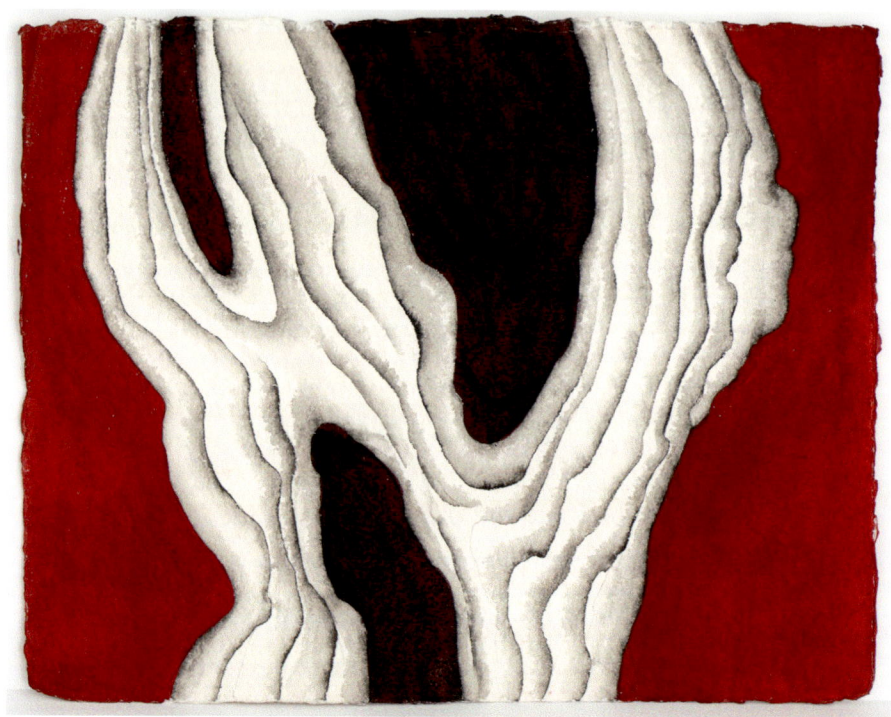

PLATE 27.
UNTITLED 1996
WATERCOLOR ON PAPER
9¾ X 12¼ IN (24.8 X 31.1 CM)

PLATE 28.
UNTITLED 1996
WATERCOLOR ON PAPER
12 X 9⅝ IN   (30.5 X 24.4 CM)

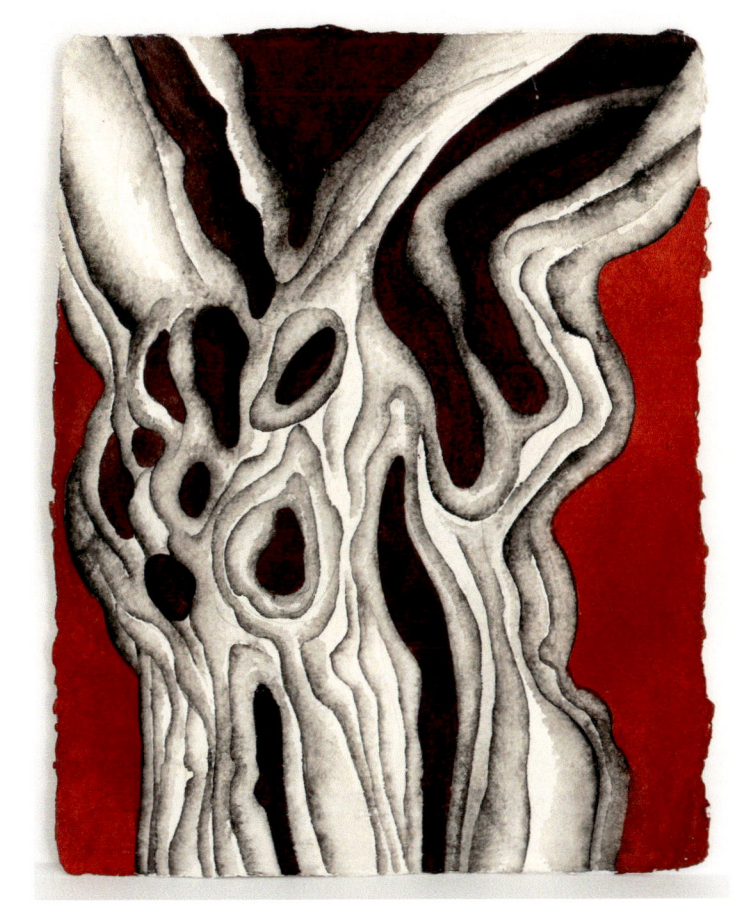

PLATE 29.
OLD APPLE III 1995
WATERCOLOR ON PAPER
12½ X 9¾ IN   (31.8 X 24.8 CM)

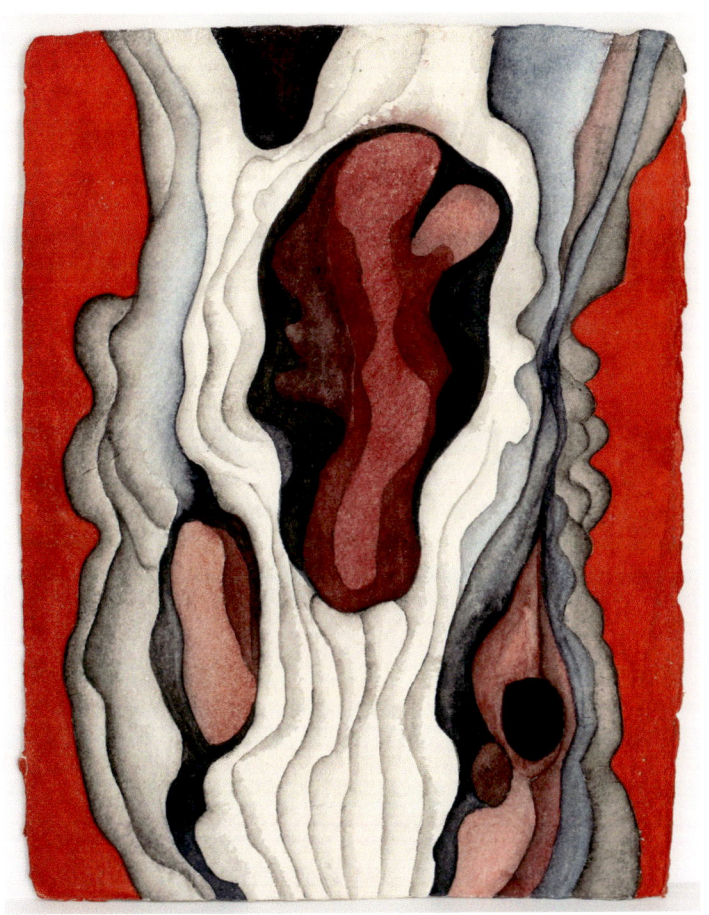

PLATE 30. **BLUE HEAD** 1997 BRONZE 20 X 12 X 6 IN (50.8 X 30.5 X 15.2 CM)

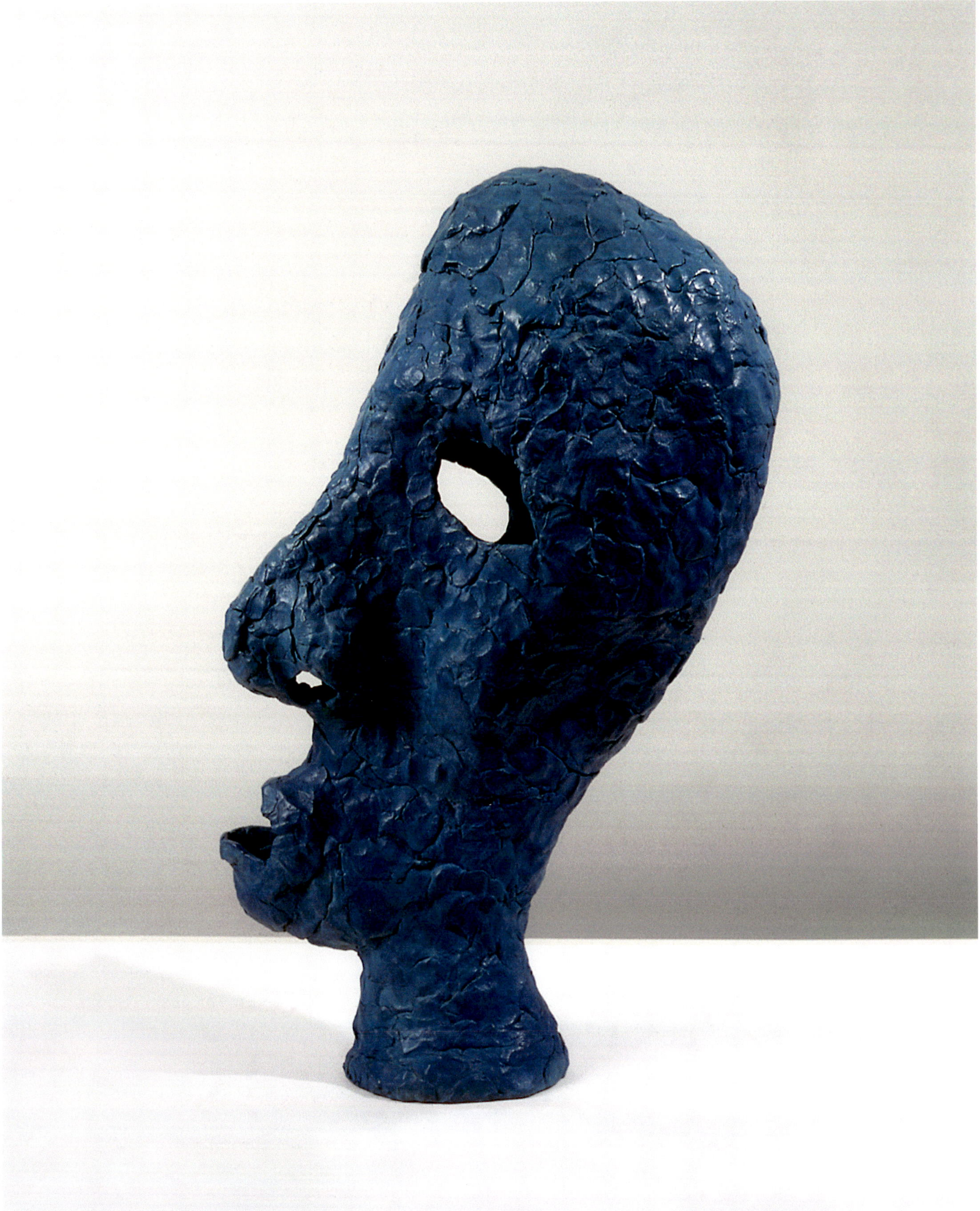

Published on the occasion of the exhibition

MARY ANN UNGER
ACROSS THE BERING STRAIT

April 17 – May 17, 2025

BERRY■CAMPBELL

524 West 26th Street
New York, NY 10001
info@berrycampbell.com
212.924.2178

View the entire exhibition online at www.berrycampbell.com

© Berry Campbell LLC, New York, 2025

All artwork images © Estate of Mary Ann Unger

"Pilgrims' Progress: Mary Ann Unger's *Across the Bering Strait*" © Glenn Adamson
"Mary Ann Unger's Microcosmic Monuments to Life" © Jess Wilcox

Designed by Mark Robinson
Photography by Adam Reich

Published by Berry Campbell LLC
Printed by GHP Media, West Haven, CT

Artwork and text in this publication is protected by copyright and may not be reproduced in any form without written request.

Every effort has been made to obtain the permission of and to acknowledge the current owners of illustrated art. Errors or omissions in credit citations or failure to obtain permission if required by copyright law have been either unavoidable or unintentional.

Photo credits:
© Estate of Eva Hesse, Courtesy Hauser & Wirth: Page 8, Figure 1.
© Vanni Archive / Art Resource / NY: Page 10, Figure 4.
Courtesy Museo Civico Sansepolcro, Arezzo, Italy: Page 25, Figure 10.
Courtesy Mary Ann Unger Estate, New York: Page 7, Figure 1, Page 9, Figures 3 and 4, Pages 12-13, Page 20, Figure 3, Page 21, Figures 4 and 5, Page 22, Figure 6, Page 23, Figure 7, Page 24, Figure 8 Figure 9, Page 25, Figure 11.

ISBN: 978-1-960708-19-9
Library of Congress Control Number: 2025905333

Cover: *Across the Bering Strait* (Detail), 1992–1994, Hydrocal over steel with cheesecloth and pigment, 72 x 660 x 396 inches (182.9 x 1676.4 x 1005.8 cm). Photo: Ryan Speth.